**monsoon**books

# LOVE ENTREPRENEURS

In 2003, British offshore finance ~~expert Phil Nicks~~ left the United Kingdom and travelled to Asia, designating Thailand his favourite country of residence. He has written several books under different brand names.

Nicks is currently researching blissful cross-culture relationships in Thailand for a new book, and contributes regularly to the relationship advisory service at *www.crossculturelove.com*.

For more information about the author, visit his website at: *www.philnicks.com*.

# ENTREPRENEURS

### Cross-culture relationship deals in Thailand

## PHIL NICKS

**monsoon**

**monsoon**books

Published in 2008
by Monsoon Books Pte Ltd
52 Telok Blangah Road
#03-05 Telok Blangah House
Singapore 098829
www.monsoonbooks.com.sg

ISBN: 978-981-05-9211-0

This book, which is the result of extensive investigative research,
offers no guarantee. There is no secret formula for success in love.
If there is such a thing as a rulebook for cross-culture relationships,
you are holding it now. Read this book; then forget everything you
have learnt, before allowing your heart to betray your mind.

Many names of characters profiled in this book have been changed
to protect their identity.

Cover photograph copyright © Collin Patrick, Black Studio
www.black.com.sg

Printed in Singapore
12 11 10 09 08            1 2 3 4 5 6 7 8 9

This book is dedicated to Love Entrepreneurs—
people who know what they want and who are
empowered to get it.

*The golden rule with cross-culture relationships is never to cross the cultural borderline; instead, meet at the cultural intersection and observe, learn and exchange. If either party attempts to change their partner, the line has been crossed.*

# CONTENTS

## PART THREE: EMERGING MARKETS

## APPENDICES

# INTRODUCTION

## The Economics of Love

It is difficult to dispute the allure of free-market global economics and it's interesting how it has taken a grip on Thailand. The Western lifestyle, which is broadcast globally, 24/7, seems to be hard to beat. Nowadays many young Thai ladies, particularly those from poorer families, make it their business to marry a foreigner; this phenomenon is the fashionable shortcut to riches.

Free market economics is not discriminating. This economic system of matching supply and demand applies to every product and service, including the provision of companionship and emotional fulfillment. Beautiful feminine and loving Thai ladies have something to offer foreign men, who cannot find what they need on their home turf. It's basically a symbiotic trade of financial security and 'lifestyle upgrade' in exchange for tender loving care—a sort of 'quid pro quo'—though it's not clear who is getting more quid for quo, or more quo for quid.

Cross-culture relationships in Thailand often resemble business deals. The Western concept of love is markedly different than the traditional Eastern way. **In Thailand love must be earned.** It's important to understand the importance of relationship economics in Thailand otherwise the 'game' is risky and sometimes dangerous. Don't expect your partner to exhibit love before you have demonstrated your ability and commitment to the partnership.

This book will take you through the process of negotiating a mutually agreeable relationship contract.

Love entrepreneurship works in many ways; not only are disadvantaged Issan girls looking for a way out, there are also hundreds of opportunistic *farang* teachers seeking lonely rich Thai ladies for marriage ... and lifestyle upgrades. There is much more happening here than meets the eye.

The following message was posted on the Thaivisa.com website:

*In the year 2004, my hometown in America registered 49 marriages and 32 divorces. Is the modern relationship of the Western world on the deathbed? An owner of a Bangkok matchmaking agency claims that oriental-style marriages have a much higher success rate than conventional Western legal marriages. I noted that just about all Thai singles' profiles specify a future husband who is 'financially secure'. Yes, the girls are looking for a provider. Maybe not all farang males want to be a provider, but I don't quite understand why this traditional role model should be so bad.*

***For me, being the provider is a far better option than constant fights with a 'liberated' woman. And long-term, it's the cheaper option too.***

*I have been fortunate. All my in-laws are hard-working and none of them drink or gamble. I did pay a dowry of $10,000 but my wife's parents wanted to return the money to us. In the end my wife suggested we give the money to her* *dad who had some debts after buying new equipment for his construction company. After my wife moved to America, we were expected to remit monthly payments to my wife's youngest sister, who needed support during her university education. Now that she has graduated, we have no further financial commitments to the family.*

The point that's being made is this: **Sure, the relationship is about money, BUT IT WORKS**. Of course there are cultural differences but they should be regarded as opportunities and not threats. A compatible socio-economic background and common relationship goals are far more important success criteria than proximity of hometowns.

## The Love Industry

The love industry is a multi-billion dollar economy, just like any other multinational industry.

This is a book about cross-border relationships; and each chapter focuses on a different aspect. Specific attention is paid to relationship economics—an integral aspect of relationships in Thailand—by an author with professional training in finance.

The framework of each chapter is built upon anecdotes arising from interviews with Thai and *farang* men and women. The book aims to highlight the key cross-cultural relationship issues and provide readers with practical tips and guidance. The guidebook offers a fusion of entertainment and subjective comment by interviewees with researched facts from multiple sources.

## Unique Selling Points

Every year, millions of men and women visit Thailand from the West seeking fulfillment. Many are survivors of traumatic marital break-ups and believe that Thailand is as good a place as any to make a new start.

Liza, a cross-culture specialist in Southeast Asia says 'I've travelled in fifty-four countries and I have probably lived in over half of them, and I found that Thai ladies are probably the prettiest, most feminine of all. I am not going to use the words "most beautiful" but they are so pleasant to look at and the most feminine. The funniest ladies are the Filipinas because of their sense of humor and their playfulness. But Thai ladies are the most feminine.'

Thailand is one of the best locations for retirees to really enjoy themselves. Not only does the dollar buy more, there is more to buy. **Thai people are among the kindest and most attentive people in the world.**

Whereas relationships tend to be increasingly standardized in the West, Southeast Asia provides limitless relationship options to suit each person's unique needs. Also, a man's age is not a limiting factor, so older men can enjoy the company of younger women without being castigated.

If a man is considerably older or physically out-of-shape, it's not a major problem from a Thai woman's perspective. Her most important requirements are that he's able and willing to offer financial support for her and her family. If he also happens to be kind and physically attractive, then that's a plus—but without ample money, the relationship is a non-starter.

Phil Nicks

Part One

# OPPORTUNITIES & DEALS

# LOVE ENTREPRENEURS

*Whenever the western man comes here, he should call me. I am
every woman for every man. I am every wife for every husband. I
am the shop with everything under one roof. Look no further!*

LOVE ENTREPRENEUR

The notion of being entrepreneurial is sexy. It's considered not only
smart but cool to be entrepreneurial, taking advantage of prevailing
opportunities. Entrepreneurs, like Richard Branson of the global
Virgin Group, are opportunists who have a knack for playing rules
and regulations to their advantage. What is the problem with applying
this same rationale to relationships?

Love Entrepreneurs comprise millions of opportunists worldwide
who benefit from cross-culture relationships. In Thailand this group
includes:

- Foreign men with young, beautiful Thai women
  to heal their emotional wounds following a nasty
  divorce;
- Foreign men looking for rich 'hi-so' (high society)
  Thai ladies to upgrade their lifestyle;

- Foreign men seeking marriage with feminine and attentive Thai ladies for tender loving care;
- Foreign men and women seeking commitment or emotional attachment;
- Foreign women seeking young Thai men as husbands;
- Foreign women seeking casual holiday encounters with Thai men;
- Thai ladies and men seeking foreign spouses for financial security for themselves and their families;
- Thai ladies offering themselves to foreigners for an instant lifestyle upgrade.

Many businesses benefit from the growing trend of people seeking partners from afar:

- Cyber-dating entrepreneurs, including, but not limited to, internet cafés in which many Thai ladies and men chat online to foreigners the world over;
- Entrepreneurial introduction agents;
- Advertising executives, who create culturally blended role models for their advertising campaigns;
- Offshoots of the pharmaceutical industry, selling skin whitening cream to Asian ladies to facilitate their East–West transformation;
- Entertainment managers, agents, bar owners, massage parlour owners and others;
- Translators, interpreters, scribes and language teachers who facilitate communication between East and West;
- Private detectives who exist to confirm your suspicions

of infidelity;

- Real estate agents who source property on behalf of newlywed Thai–*farang* couples;
- The fashion industry which is driven by mass craving for physical attraction.

The shortcut to enhanced materialism is endemic. 'We want it, and we want it *now*!' is the today's cognitive byword. While the Buddhist monks live in the present moment, the people who are considered smart take advantage of opportunities in the 'now' moment. One chance meeting with a wealthy foreign man (or woman) can instantly turn a person into a millionaire—US dollars, not Thai baht.

An increasing number of Thai ladies are specifically looking for foreign men to upgrade their lifestyle, secure their family's needs and give up working. Boon, a Bangkok taxi driver, refers to this phenomenon as 'the shortcut'; it's the fast-track way for poor rural farmers' daughters to amass riches within weeks. It's legal and many Thai women consider it to be exciting. The downside is the potential loss of cultural allegiance, but dignity doesn't pay the bills.

Western men are attracted to Thailand because they can be 'more equal than others' here. He enjoys his time with his lady. When he wakes up he finds his trousers and shirt washed and pressed and his shoes are shiny! He thinks, This is nice! This never happened before back home. And so, after a few more trouser pressings, he is hooked. Then he hears himself say, involuntarily: 'Hey, I love you! Why don't we just get together and get married?'

Most Thai women want older men because they are more secure economically and are able to spend more time with them than younger men. They are also more chivalrous, polite and socially adept, and some women complain that the younger men make them work too hard in the bedroom. In short, older men tend to provide more and demand less than younger men.

Liza, a cross-culture relationship consultant, hears the following story constantly: 'I want a new life ... I want a way out ... Why not? I don't have to invest anything. I was born with this body, these looks and femininity. I don't do any harm to anyone; in fact I make him feel better. What's wrong with that?'

## THE TREND

Vanessa Broughton has been hosting a sports day at a school in Udon Thani (Issan, in Northeast Thailand) for the last ten years. The children are between kindergarten and fourth grade. Every year the event features a beauty contest and the winner of the beauty pageant, Miss Sports Day, is interviewed on stage.

Ten years ago, Miss Sports Day was asked how she enjoyed school and what she wanted to do with her life. When Vanessa asked the cute nine-year-old girl why she wanted to be an air hostess, the girl replied, 'Because only rich people get on airplanes.' Fast forward ten years and the current Miss Sports Day's answer to the same question was 'I want to be a *farang* wife.' Many Thai ladies in Northeast Thailand want to marry a *farang* as a way towards attaining financial security.

Issan, the northeastern province of Thailand, has been a breeding ground for cross-culture marriages for many years. However, the phenomenon is extending to other parts of Thailand, notably to North Thailand, and the ladies tend to be more educated than before.

# FAST-TRACK CAREER

## For Thai Women

Annie has a top management position with a foreign company, earning US$6,000 per month. She drives a smart Mercedes, but still she says: 'It's not enough. I want to a penthouse. I want to visit Europe for a week every two months'. Her girlfriend Pom, on the other hand, is a career housewife.

Annie has decided to follow Pom's career path because Annie's foreign employer has a glass ceiling on her earning capacity. In Annie's mind, her best option toward fulfilling her dreams is to marry an older wealthy man. Pom agrees with Annie's change of plan: 'Such a man is willing to give her what she wants. She doesn't love him. She doesn't want to be with him but that's the price she has to pay for upgrading her lifestyle.'

Although Annie shows affection to her partner, she doesn't really love him. She has convinced him that she cares for him but deep down she may not want to stay with him. She chooses to live a lie, because that's what it takes to upgrade her lifestyle.

## For *Farang* Men

According to Vanessa Tan, there are a growing number of *farang* English teachers seeking relationships with wealthy Thai ladies in Bangkok. These male predators can be found at five-star hotels, exclusive clubs and expat associations. Popular meeting places include The British Club, Bangkok Young Professionals' events, Rotary Clubs, Toastmasters, Round Table, interest groups, charity events and fashion shows.

Typically, a thirty-year-old teacher from UK might meet a classy

Thai lady at a social event in Bangkok. She may be overweight and lonely so when the *farang* show special interest in her, it might lead to marriage. For the foreign teacher, this could mean an upgrade from a US$150-per-month studio to a multi-million-dollar house with twelve servants and a personal driver.

## NEGOTIATIONS

Mick Andrews sent an email to a beautiful lady on an online dating site, asking her if she would have sex with him for US$100,000. She replied within ten minutes with a curt 'Yes'. Then Mick sent her another email, asking her whether she would have sex with him for US$5. She immediately phoned him and angrily asked him, 'What kind of lady do you think I am?' Mick Andrews, who claims he was only joking, said he just wanted to negotiate an affordable price.

## THE LAUNDRY

Graham Moon is a Bangkok business broker and advisor. One morning Graham received a phone call from a charming young Thai lady called Nok. After introducing herself she said she wanted to know how she could pay tax. Graham was surprised by her request but nevertheless agreed to meet her that afternoon.

At the appointed hour, two Thai ladies arrived at Graham's office.

Nok arrived with her girlfriend Pom. They both wore short skirts and blouses which revealed their midriffs. Pom had a silver ring through her pierced navel. Nok carried a large pink handbag with a bear's face on it.

After completing the customer registration form, Graham asked them why they wanted to pay taxes. He explained that most of his clients wanted to avoid paying taxes, their request was unusual.

Nok explained that her American boyfriend sends her US$500 every month from California. She said she wanted to visit Germany but she was unable to obtain a holiday visa without proof of income and evidence of payment of taxes. Graham noticed she didn't mention her American boyfriend in connection with her travel plans.

Nok receives tax-free income from her doting boyfriend in America. However the German Embassy asked for proof of salary and income tax receipts. She said she had an idea to start up a Thai limited company offering search engine optimization (SEO) services to international clients.

Nok and Pom proposed to be the company directors and major shareholders, and their boyfriends—or customers—would transfer money into their company bank account. They, as company directors, would pay themselves a salary for management services to the company.

Graham incorporated their company, Freebird Marketing Co., Ltd, and after just four salary payments they obtained holiday visas for Germany. Ever since, their company has been thriving and the cheeky little birds are constantly flying between the States, Europe and Australia on company business.

## THE VISA RUNNERS

According to Samantha Peters, many Thai ladies enter Singapore on a thirty-day transit visa and then fly on to Hong Kong, where they can also obtain a transit visa. They alternate between living in Singapore and Hong Kong, both places where they can meet high net worth men with lots of disposable income.

Samantha Peters, who regularly visits nightclubs in Hong Kong and Singapore, says she sees the same Thai ladies in both countries: 'I see these girls in a club in Hong Kong one week and then in a Singapore club a month later. Usually they operate as freelancers for a while until they get recruited by organisations which will sponsor them.'

These Thai women have a rare ability to learn languages. For example, many Thai ladies who live in Hong Kong manage to speak fluent Cantonese within a few months. In Thailand, learning the English language is viewed by many Thais as a passport to a new lifestyle.

Samantha Peters continues: 'Freelancers in Hong Kong dress well and look great. Some of them hang out in five-star hotels, drinking champagne with their friends. They communicate well and many have bachelor's degrees.'

## THE BIG SECRET

Some Thais believe that respectable Thai ladies would not stoop to being in a relationship with a foreign man. *Farang* have a reputation for liking dark-skinned women from Northeast Thailand, whereas most self-respecting Thai men prefer ladies who have paler skin.

Generally, *farang* are viewed by Thais as being crass and unrefined, and there is a lot of supporting evidence to be found on the streets of Pattaya or along Patong Beach in Phuket.

Jayson commented on *StickmanBangkok.com*, 'I've noticed that it's almost pointless to be a good-looking *farang* guy in Thailand, because you're going to have access to the same pool of women as that obese, hairy, smelly, fifty-five-year-old bald guy sitting at the end of the bar ...'

---

**Case Study: Barry Green and Nee**

Briton Barry Green is sixty years old. He recently married Nee, a beautiful twenty-seven-year-old lady from the Lahu tribe in North Thailand. Barry retired to Thailand three years ago after a career in teaching and youth work. Nee separated from her common-law Thai husband who fathered her two children, aged six and eleven.

Barry explains that they experienced a rocky ride during the initial stages of their relationship. Shortly after meeting Nee, Barry felt coerced into buying her a gold chain on a joint shopping trip. Shortly afterwards Barry made the classic mistake of buying a bar for his girlfriend to manage; the bar lost money and he nearly lost his girlfriend in the process.

It took nearly two years for Nee to develop strong feelings for Barry. Barry built a house for her on her family's land. He also purchased ten *rai* (four acres) of land for her father, enabling him to make a living by growing tea and coffee. Barry's 'good heart' (*jai dee*) enabled him to win Nee's heart in the end. Upon the advice of a local fortune-teller, Nee changed her first name and adopted Barry's family name.

Barry gifted a dowry of US$3,000 to Nee's parents before legally marrying her at an *amphur* office. Like many Thai ladies, Nee protested adamantly when Barry asked her to sign a prenuptial agreement but despite cries of 'You don't trust

---

me!' she eventually signed on the dotted line. For a specimen prenuptial agreement, see page 280.

A major issue for Barry is Nee's tendency to keep secrets, particularly about her previous lovers. It is customary in Thailand for people to refrain from saying things which may hurt another person's feelings. Barry is also very aware of what are acceptable boundaries in the relationship and enforces them whenever necessary.

### Conclusion

Barry is generous and kind to his wife and her family. He does not try to control his wife or limit her freedom (unlike many *farang*). Both Barry and Nee enjoy a sense of humour together and some independence. Barry is making the most of his retirement, and good luck to him!

## ARE YOU ENTREPRENEURIAL?

Or are you really trafficking your spouse? Because there are feminists out there who believe that some 'economically unbalanced' marriages fall within the definition of sexual trafficking.

The following is an extract from 'Human Trafficking and United Nations Peacekeeping DPKO Policy Paper (March 2004)':

*An agreed definition of human trafficking now exists under Article 3 of the 'Palermo Protocol' on trafficking in persons, which has come into force on 25 December 2003. This internationally agreed definition focuses on exploitation of human beings—be it for sexual exploitation, other forms of forced labour, slavery, servitude, or for the removal of human organs. Trafficking takes place by criminal means through the threat or use of force, coercion, abduction, fraud, deception, abuse of positions of power or abuse of positions of vulnerability. It relates to all stages of the trafficking process: recruitment, transportation, transfer, harbouring or receipt of persons. Trafficking is not just a transnational crime across international borders—the definition applies to internal domestic trafficking of human beings.*

There are potentially millions of married couples worldwide, who are included in the above United Nations definition of trafficking. If a Thai lady is vulnerable, due to poverty or otherwise, and she agrees to sign a marriage contract with a wealthy foreign man (in a position of power) and his support is conditional upon their interaction together, some feminists might say he is trafficking his wife.

What such feminists don't take into account is that, although the lady may be doing certain things she doesn't really enjoy, she regards it as her career and obligation to her family; and she appreciates the enhanced financial security and lifestyle that goes with it. If a 'career marriage' is really a job for a poor lady, consider that a minority of employees are genuinely passionate about their work.

According to Romyen Kosaiyakanon of Chiang Mai University's Women's Studies Centre, some traditional feminists may even consider online dating as a modern form of cross-border sex trade. Romyen completed a research project entitled *Cross-Border Marriages: A Case Study of Thai Women-Foreign Men Matches Through Online Dating Services in Thailand.*

If online dating is trafficking in women, it is more sophisticated than other forms. Foreign men have more power than the Thai women in terms of wealth, supply and demand. There are six times as many women as there are men using online dating systems.

If trafficking boils down to economic servitude—or free market economics—surely any employer contracting with staff that does not enjoy their work is guilty. Is the office cleaner genuinely enjoying his or her job, or just doing it for the money (like a prostitute)? If sex work is real work, then relevant discussion points are economic reward, conditions and environment of the work.

## SUMMARY

- Love Entrepreneurs will find you, so you don't need to look for them;
- Love Entrepreneurs comprise Thais, *farang* men and women, and businessmen all over the world;
- The ladies of Northeast Thailand, who have lower social status, tend to be most interested in marrying *farang* men to secure their family interests;
- Many proper Thai ladies would not seriously consider having a romantic relationship with *farang*;
- Thai men tend to prefer young Thai ladies (under thirty years of age) with pale skin and commensurate social status;
- The ad execs are stimulating interest in cross-culture relationships by using fashion models (and pop stars like Tata Young) that depict a blend of East and West.

# LOVE CONTRACTS

*Relationships—particularly cross-culture partnerships with Thais—are all about deals; and to establish a mutually agreeable relationship contract, the couple requires negotiation and communication skills.*

Harmonious relationships often depend upon negotiated contractual agreements between the couple and subsequent monitoring, review and revision of the terms of agreement. Most harmonious cross-culture relationships are based upon an agreed 'love contract' between the partners. These contracts are similar to a business partnership agreement but much more complex because there are so many other factors to consider than just money.

These agreements are especially important in cross-culture relationships because the expectations of each party are not only different but easily misunderstood by each partner. The parties to the agreement have different cultural beliefs and needs, and there may be communication issues if they are not both fluent in a common language. The criteria for a successful cross-culture relationship are:

- A negotiated relationship 'deal' between the two parties to the contract;
- The deal needs to be clearly communicated and

understood by each party;

- The agreement should cover all possible foreseeable events;
- Ideally the contract should be written in both languages and signed by both parties so neither party can deny their agreement in future;
- The contract should cover the possibility of breach of contract and dissolution of the partnership;
- The relationship should be evaluated (by reference to the contract) on a periodic basis.

If no relationship contract has been discussed or written each party will have their own 'deemed contracts', which are usually incompatible with one another. For example, a Thai lady may start a relationship with a foreign man thinking that he will support her and her family financially. The foreign man may assume she is financially dependent because she has a job. Her family may expect more money to flow their way because she is in a relationship with a supposedly rich *farang*. If her family becomes resentful, the relationship could experience additional tensions.

## CROSS-CULTURE LOVE CONTRACTS

According to Susan Smith, a cross-culture relationship counselor based in Asia, every relationship has deals that need to be communicated clearly to both parties. Says Susan, 'These deals can be amended, shortened, lengthened or whatever.'

# HOW TO ESTABLISH A LOVE CONTRACT

Before establishing a love contract it is necessary for both parties to express what they want from the relationship and what they can offer to strengthen the partnership. Ideally, each party balances their taking with giving.

For a valid love contract, both parties need to know themselves and be open about what they want. It is advantageous to use a professional mediator to push for answers to awkward questions, possibly about sex or money. Thai women often feel shy talking directly about such personal matters.

These contracts exist in some form or other even if they are not discussed.

## TYPES OF CONTRACT

Love contracts may be standard legal marriage contracts, local village matrimonial ceremonies or customized contracts. The deals may be assumed, spoken or written. Most relationship contracts are a combination of spoken, assumed and marriage agreements.

### Pay-As-You-Go (PAYG) Contracts

PAYG relationships are short-time contracts between consenting adults. Many bars and entertainment venues provide an environment for men to enjoy short periods of intimacy with women.

These short-term contracts are quite straightforward: The lady flatters the customer (telling a few porky pies along the way) and tells him how sexy he is. The customer gets excited and throws money at her. For this contract to work well, both parties keep it light and have fun with each other.

Relationships are like railway journeys. It is possible to travel the entire route by the same train—say from Moscow to Beijing— or travel to the next station and change trains. Why commit to a destination before you know where you want to stay?

PAYG relationships suit people who have low earnings. They also suit people in emotional tatters who are in between serious relationships. This type of encounter is always up for grabs by anyone who wants a variety of fun without the commitments.

According to Buddhist philosophy, emotional attachment is the cause of pain and suffering. PAYG relationships bypass emotional attachment. The objective is light-hearted entertainment: fun without suffering afterwards.

One prerequisite for harmonious PAYG relationships is mutual respect for each other. This means keeping your promises and being responsible for their welfare during the agreed term of the encounter.

Barry Sandal wrote an 'idiot's guide' to PAYG relationships in Thailand entitled *Foreign Relations*, which is intended as a primer to help foreigners avoid the usual pitfalls. The author heard of so many people losing their money, homes and more that he wrote a simple concise set of guidelines (with illustrations) to brief, entertain and forewarn newcomers.

Barry designed the book using hand-drawn illustrations and large text. Says Barry: 'In my mind I saw a foreigner sitting on the beach in Pattaya, beer in hand, a little buzzed already, reading the book and laughing. He would be thinking "Ohmygod, I just did that!" It's lighthearted and simple, but all the messages are there.'

Barry Sandal's golden rules for PAYG relationships are: Come to Asia and be happy! Smile! If you've agreed to pay some money, pay it. Don't make a problem. Don't break the law. Then go home unmarried. Don't fall in love. Don't buy them a house or a car.

Says Barry: 'These girls are not stupid but they are uneducated. So after a couple of hours, there may not be much to talk about. You can't talk about sports or politics, and even if you want to talk about something local, she probably comes from Issan, far away.'

For more information about PAYG contracts, see 'Opportunities in the Food & Beverage Industry' and 'Pay-As-You-Go-Love'.

### The Monthly Retainer

Some guys pay their girlfriends a monthly retainer for exclusive contact with them whenever they visit their country.

Says Barry Sandal: 'I know a guy called Brett who pays his woman US$2,500 each month. She stays with him whenever he's in the country (about four months each year). Then she goes with every Thai guy as soon as he leaves. Brett treats her like a pet and she does everything to please him. Brett really doesn't care what she gets up to when he's outside the country. That's the contract.'

Their contract states that she must do whatever Brett wants whenever he is in Thailand. And he may give her an hour's notice. So she is always on standby for Brett. As soon as he's in town she has to drop all of her other plans or interests.

There is no love in Brett's arrangement. She wants Brett's money and Brett wants a cute pet to play with. The two Love Entrepreneurs have negotiated a working relationship.

### The Courtesans

There are agencies in Asia providing really professional courtesans.

One punter spent US$175 baht for an escort to visit him one evening and she wouldn't sleep with him. This lady was in such high demand that she was booked for three months ahead—every week with a different client.

The lady was really hot and she knew her job. For the seven days she is with her customer, she is the perfect girlfriend: classy, well dressed, polite and a pleasure to be with. She could easily pass for the girlfriend of a wealthy businessman. And she probably earns around US$80 per day.

## RELATIONSHIP CONTRACTS

Relationship contracts are agreements made between two people to define the terms of engagement and clarify the responsibilities of both parties. These contracts may be for a specific or indefinite period of time. If the contract is for a specific period there is usually an option for renewal of the agreement.

Relationship contracts may be standard (as in marriages) or customized. Both types of relationship contract are between two parties. Matrimonial contracts are usually registered with a governmental organization. Customized relationship contracts do not have to be registered with any official organization.

Relationship contracts can be documented, ceremonial, spoken or etheric in nature. Documented contracts are normally signed by both parties and their witnesses on the date of agreement. Thai wedding ceremonies establish a relationship contract with a set of assumed responsibilities for both parties.

An etheric (or ethereal) relationship contract is usually intrinsic to the circumstances of the initial meeting of the two parties. For example, if a hostess meets a client in a bar there is an implied contract of service between them. Once a contract has been established in this way it can be difficult, if not impossible, to change it.

There are many benefits of creating a renewable short-term relationship contract (from one hour to one year), especially at the beginning of a relationship when the partners are getting to know one another. The main purpose is to avoid misunderstandings and unfulfilled expectations.

It is advisable to use a professional mediator (or relationship facilitator) to develop the agreement and monitor the progress of the couple. Without an impartial third-party facilitator there is a tendency for couples to avoid difficult issues. For example, many couples settle for an inadequate sex life because they feel uncomfortable discussing these issues. A mediator would draw attention to such matters and support them through resolution of the issues.

Typical components of a relationship contract include:

- The date of the agreement;
- The period of the agreement and options for renewal;
- Sexual behaviour: sexual hygiene, birth control, sexual identity and deviations, frequency of medical examinations, fidelity, minimum frequency, quality enhancement (see Children);
- Finance and economy: for both parties and the combined entity: income, savings, debt, pensions, insurance, property, wills, financial commitments, businesses, family support;
- Personal development: skills development, hobbies and interests, vocational education, retreats, spiritual

practices, reading, seminars and workshops;

- Family commitments: time and money to support all members of both families, private and public holidays, Birthdays and festivals;
- Mediation: a periodic relationship health check-up by an impartial professional to facilitate the development of the relationship entity;
- Children: family planning, education, responsibilities of both parties to the children;
- Dissolution: arrangements to be made in the event of dissolution of the relationship contract, including responsibilities for children, apportionment of property between the two parties;
- Personal friends: definition of personal boundaries and what external friendships are acceptable;
- Death: wills and funeral arrangements if either party dies;
- Time together: define minimum acceptable periods of time together;
- Sickness: responsibility to take care of each other (and both children and family members) in the event of sickness.

---

### Case Study

Bangkok businessman Harry is open with his friends about being bisexual. He is married to a Thai lady, some twenty years younger than himself. They own a house in Surin and a flat in

---

Bangkok. Harry's wife works on the family farm. Harry and his wife are apart a lot of the time because she is so busy farming.

When Harry meets a *katoey*, he will explain that he is happily married and has no intention of changing that. Once he has clarified his situation, he continues, 'Now let's have a good time!'

Harry's deal with his wife is quite normal in Thailand. He provides her some security and a real commitment. He is allowed to philander a little bit, as long as it's safe and there's no emotional attachment.

Says Harry about his wife: 'We've known each other now for fifteen years. We've been married four and a half years, so we knew each other a long time before we got married. In fact, she didn't think I was ever going to ask her and she wouldn't tell anybody for days after I proposed. She kept coming back to me, "Are you sure? Are you sure?" She didn't want to tell people—she was afraid I was going to change my mind. It's the best thing I ever did.'

Harry describes his wife's family as wonderful. 'They're rice farmers from the Northeast and not in the least bit dysfunctional. I wish my family had been that together.

'There's no conflict between my lifestyle and my marriage. I wouldn't allow that. If it wasn't OK with my wife, I wouldn't be sitting here giving you this interview. I've always been open with my friends.'

# BREACH OF CONTRACT

Try to avoid breaking your relationship contracts. Breaching relationship contracts in Thailand can be an especially risky business.

---

### Case Study: Termination Contracts

John is American. He broke up with his Thai wife, Nok, recently. His wife demanded a reasonable settlement to compensate her for the broken contract. John refused to cooperate. Nok trashed his name throughout town.

During the subsequent three months Nok received no fewer than four contractual offers by freelance assassins to kill John. Two of the quotes were as low as US$150. Fortunately for John, Nok did not pursue that option.

---

### Case Study: Eating Out

According to Susan Smith, some wealthy Thai ladies are attracted to *farang* men because they treat them well and lavish them with attention. In one case, the foreign man, David, was married to a rich Thai lady called Law. Susan asked him: 'Your wife is perfect in everybody's eyes, so why would you want to go with that other girl?' He replied 'When we come home and open the fridge and find there is not much food in there, we go shopping. We buy the things we don't have at home.'

Says Susan, 'It's so simple, isn't it? It struck me right in

---

my heart. I started to think about all the things we cannot get at home. But do the people at home know exactly what you like, and do you know exactly what you like?' So many people are quick to break their contract and go on shopping sprees elsewhere. Susan asks David 'Do you have to go out and buy things all the time? Are you demanding different things all the time, or is it always the same thing which is not available at home any more?'

Law hired a private detective to keep David under surveillance. She wanted to know which women David dated and where they went. Law was so preoccupied with her unfaithful husband that she had no time for her children.

Once, when Susan met Law, Law's daughter phoned and asked for some pizza. Law shouted into the phone, 'For God's sake, go and get it yourself! I'm not a bloody pizza company!' Shortly afterwards Law spent thirty minutes talking to her private detective (who had previously admitted to Susan that he makes up many of his investigation reports) ... Meanwhile her children are still hungry.

### Case Study: Sex for English Lessons

Author Barry Sandal's first girlfriend in Thailand was a teacher. He met her on a bus. Barry never paid her any money and he didn't buy her anything. In fact Barry even loaned her some money which she repaid. Says Barry, 'It was an interesting deal: Sex for English.'

He continues, 'She wanted to work as an au pair in the States, and she needed someone to help her with her job application. So I helped her appear more educated than she really was. I edited all her application forms to a reasonable standard of English. She got in! She was even accepted for a second year. Then she got married to an American man. Bye! Bye!'

## SUMMARY

- The key to successful cross-culture relationships is the negotiation of love contracts and clear communication of each party's relationship goals;
- Always stick to the deal you made at the beginning, otherwise there may be trouble;
- If you have US$2,000 to spare why not enjoy a really classy girlfriend for a week—but you may have to wait three months because she is in great demand!

# WHERE FOREIGN WOMEN FIND LOVE

*The belief that women are less promiscuous than men is ridiculous when you consider who men are being promiscuous with.*

JAMES BRADLEY

*Whenever my dad is in town, everyone thinks he is my boyfriend— how disgusting is that?*

A THAI LADY WHO HAS A FARANG FATHER

Many *farang* women who reside in Thailand complain about feeling invisible to both Thai and *farang* men. Lots of *farang* men stay in Thailand to escape from *farang* women, described by one man as mobile refrigeration units; others have had no success with relationships in their home country. Although Thai men are often too shy to approach *farang* women, there are plenty of dating opportunities for *farang* women with local guides and beach boys, and some *farang* women do find true love with an Thai partner.

Lady journalist Lyle Walter observes that Thai guys think *farang* women are too big (or fat), too sweaty and too loud to be appealing. Lyle doesn't receive second glances in Bangkok; there's just too much competition from sexier, more feminine Thai Goddesses. Lyle's rant is available at: *http://www.lylesinrodwalter.blogs.com.*

In Thailand there are three main types of relationships available to foreign women:

- Casual friendships with local guides, especially on the islands;
- Serious relationships with Thai men, including those from the hill-tribes of North Thailand;
- Short-time encounters with male sex workers.

There are several escort agencies which service women in Bangkok. They charge up to US$300 per night. Male prostitutes in Bangkok are attracting more female customers. Dr Suporn Koentsawang, President of the Quality of Life Development association says, 'We are very interested to see the increasing business of males selling sex to females.' In a survey of male prostitutes, eighty-four percent said they offered their services to both men and women.

From an international perspective, Kenya, Botswana and Ghana are the most popular destinations for female sex tourists, though Southeast Asia is gaining in popularity. Recent reports estimate that one in five wealthy female travellers in Kenya seek African men for recreational gratification.

There are a growing number of genuinely serious relationships between Asian men and *farang* women. In this chapter there is a profile of a cross-culture marriage between a British woman and a young man from the Karen tribe in Northern Thailand.

Another large group of foreign women who visit Thailand for (paid) sexual fulfillment are middle class Chinese Malaysians, Chinese Singaporean and Japanese women. An expat in Singapore comments: 'I knew of several Chinese Malaysian and Singaporean girls who went on package tours to Thailand and asked their tour guides to find them men. This was a paid service. I presume the men usually offered their services to other men. None of the girls seemed to enjoy the experience. Japanese girls often travel to Southeast Asia for sex; it's pretty common, especially in Bali and Thailand.'

---

**Case Study:**

**A Day in the life of a *farang* woman in Thailand**

American Vicky Reynolds has lived in Thailand for eight years. Vicky shares her experience as a single *farang* woman living in Thailand.

**About Thai Men**

Some women enjoy dating Thai men because often they pay for everything and don't expect sex. One *farang* woman dated a Thai man for four years without sex. Also Thai men provide for their families financially. Her husband gives her almost all of his pay check, and just keeps some light pocket money.

Thai men do know that *farang* women are going to 'put out' much easier than Thai women, so the ones who are interested in *farang* women probably take that into account. Another reason is that *farang* woman return home eventually, so he has no commitment, and can therefore move onto new sex partners.

Thais are not into oral sex either. All my Thai girlfriends and *farang* girlfriends say that Thai men almost never perform oral sex and there's very little foreplay. Thai girls don't like to give oral sex but the men don't want it either—probably

---

because they are concerned about cleanliness. Karen men are circumcised though and most women prefer that.

Few Thai men are divorced or single past the age of thirty because most marry early and stay with their family, even though they might cheat a bit. So *farang* women over twenty-five years old have fewer chances to meet suitable Thai men. Many *farang* women date Thai guys younger than themselves though, sometimes a decade younger.

### Single *Farang* Women

It seems for both genders the notion of finding a partner, a true equal, is too hard. Most people are dating Thais for the sex and physical intimacy, and using Western friends to fill in the gaps of conversation. It takes a very confident *farang* woman to live in Thailand as a single woman.

If you can be secure in yourself and live on your own and be happy, then this is the place for you. But if you are a woman who needs a partnership with a man and needs men to make you feel good about yourself, you will hate Thailand. *Farang* men are less interested in *farang* women, and Thai men can be shy.

### Social Class

Many *farang* women go with dark Thai guys with dreadlocks—men who no self-respecting Thai lady would want to meet.

I would get hit on every day of the week in the USA or Australia, but in Thailand, not even once. Of course there's social class to consider in Thailand, which is something I would not need to consider in the USA. In the States it does not matter what someone does for a living.

If I were to date a Thai, it would not be a dreadlocked bar boy because that would be scraping the bottom of the social barrel - and that's not me being snotty—it's about the culture. It's acceptable in the States, but it's not acceptable here. It's better for me to be an old maid here, than to date someone who is a plumber—but in the USA a plumber is considered a great job.

### Infidelity

Thais are often accepting of cheating. Some women turn a blind eye to infidelity if the man is discreet and continues to provide security for her; others break up with their philandering spouses.

The consensus among women is that 'A man is like a dog. If you give him steak to eat, he will still eat shit, and come back to lick your face.' however, many Thai women think that *farang* men are completely faithful ... and we know that's not true.

### Alternative Technology

It's interesting that Thailand, a country known for fulfilment of sensory desire, renders female sex toys illegal. Nearly every woman who has a connection with the outside world has smuggled a vibrator into the country.

## POPULAR MEETING PLACES IN THAILAND

Thailand's islands are popular scouting grounds for *farang* women seeking lust and adventure. Favourite places for single *farang* women to meet young Thai studs include Koh Samet, Koh Pha Ngan and Koh Phi Phi.

Sally Reynolds sums up her experience, 'Thai men are incredibly charming, kind and considerate; they even carry my bags and open the door for me, unlike *farang* guys. Even if you're not going to walk down the aisle with [a Thai guy], they are definitely worth a holiday romance.'

Chiang Mai is a popular destination for *farang* woman to take their sabbatical and spend their alimony check. Alimony goes a long way in Chiang Mai, and there are plenty of spas to wash away any lingering memories of ex-him.

There is no age limit for women who procure the services of young Thai men. A seventy-year-old woman, who lives in Northern Thailand, hired a young guy to have sex with her for 150 baht (US$4). Her daughter walked into her room and thought she was being raped so she called the police. Later the old woman had to explain to the police that she had paid the guy for sex.

## TOY BOYS

Empowered Western women are opting for ever younger men to spice up their love lives. According to an AARP survey on sexuality among single Americans aged between forty and sixty-nine, thirty-five percent of women want to date younger men, and thirty-four percent actually do so.

# BEACH BOYS, PLAYBOYS, GIGOLOS

Several young Thai men were interviewed about their relationships with *farang* women. These guys are typically aged in their thirties, speak English reasonably well and have a penchant for partying (*sanook*).

Sam says of the female *farang* sex tourists, 'They are butterflies. They like to try men from every country: Africa, The Caribbean, Asia ... and now it's fashionable for *farang* women to go with Thai men'. Many of the Thai men have been hurt by *farang* women who profess true love for them, and who quickly disappear without a word. Sam says that many Thai guys feel 'used' by foreign sex tourists; after five or so such encounters, they cannot trust *farang* women any more.

In Thailand, men are more equal than women. Sam proudly says that he always protects his woman; she will always be safe in his company. These charming men are macho and attentive; they are also known for being very jealous too.

According to Sam, the real Thai gigolos, known as beach boys (or *dek goh*), work on the islands in the south of Thailand. A popular place for the *farang* women to enjoy brief encounters with macho Thai men is Haad Rin, on the island of Koh Pha Ngan. Other popular resorts for female sex tourists include Koh Lanta, Krabi and Koh Phi Phi.

The main difference between male and female sex tourism lies in the exchange; female sex tourism is low-key and usually the Thai men will spend time with the women in exchange for the cost of food and drinks (and sometimes tips or gifts). Usually *farang* women do not have to pay for it, whereas male sex tourists would be expected to pay for female companionship.

For further information about the experiences of foreign women in Thailand, refer to the ThaiVisa.com community forum for foreign women or Thailandqa.com (*http://www.thailandqa.com*).

## COMMITTED RELATIONSHIPS

A common obstacle to commitment in relationships by *farang* women to Thai men is infidelity and the cultural belief that men are 'more equal' than women in Thailand. The majority of *farang* women, therefore, prefer casual encounters with Thais.

Tanya Greenhalgh, who lives in Vancouver, made the following comment: 'I had a relationship with an Asian man and I concluded that a relationship with someone whose core beliefs differ from mine is not workable. For example, fidelity is something I expect from a committed relationship but people from other cultures have different expectations. Many Asian men go to brothels. I'm certainly not saying the Western world has it all figured out—in fact I'm sure it hasn't—but I'm not likely to change certain beliefs, nor do I expect anyone else to do so. That's the first core belief that jumped out at me, and I'm sure there are others. Just not interested in going there again; same-culture relationships are hard enough!'

Aussie 'Cat' summarises her experience with her Thai boyfriend: 'I dated a poor farm boy from Issan who had a low paid job in Bangkok. He was uneducated but sweet and polite. His English was OK but we spoke Thai mostly. We enjoyed eating Thai food (or pizza) and watching movies together. We had a really good sex life, unadventurous but very satisfying. He fell in love with me quickly; I told him to take it slowly. It seemed strange for me to be in the position of power in the relationship because I was the rich one.

'He wanted me to make all the decisions: where to hang out, what to eat or do. My job entails me to make decisions all day so I got sick of always hearing "It's up to you!" I didn't love him as much as he loved me so I couldn't take him seriously, knowing that he would not survive in Australia with me if we stayed together.'

Cat says she finds Thai men very attractive physically (with beautiful skin), handsome, caring, neat and clean, and funny. However, Cat considers Thai men to be less confident than *farang* men. Sometimes she felt uncomfortable when they were seen together in public, because people assume he is a gigolo, bar boy or toy boy.

Cat concludes, 'In the beginning I liked that we didn't talk much—it was a rest from the demands of my job—but after a while it got frustrating that we couldn't discuss anything more profound than what we should eat for lunch. If we were financial equals it might work better.'

---

**Case Study: Sandra and Chalerm**

There are several British women living in Chiang Mai who had successful careers in UK and who are now married to hill tribe men from North Thailand. These women make no secret that they enjoy being in control. Their lifestyles in Southeast Asia allow them to have fun and pamper their young good-looking partners. And most of them seem very happy.

Sandra, an accomplished project manager from UK, met her Karen (a hill tribe) husband, Chalerm, when she visited Thailand alone during 2004. Chalerm, who is seven years younger than Sandra, was her tour guide. Sandra describes their first meeting as 'love at first sight'.

---

Chalerm, who has a reasonable command of English, was educated at a high school by missionaries; he has difficulty dealing with Sandra whenever she argues with him; usually he responds by getting upset and being morose. Sandra has elected to take financial responsibility for their household.

Sandra and Chalerm have completely 'tied the knot': not only do they have a child together, they have participated in three wedding ceremonies. The first ceremony was the legal marriage at an *amphur* office; the second was the traditional Karen village ceremony (detailed below); and finally they had a traditional Christian blessing at a church in England.

Sandra received full maternity pay from her Thai employer for forty-five days; then the social security fund paid her a lower amount for a further forty-five days.

Sandra assists Chalerm with ideas and finance for his new trekking business. She says she is prepared to downsize in future if necessary; it would entail renting out their house, and living in Chalerm's Karen village. To make that transition, they would have to live on Chalerm's income, which is currently one quarter of Sandra's.

Karen hill tribes span the width of Southeast Asia. One of the oldest Karen settlements in Northern Thailand originated in Myanmar. The Karen tribes have their own languages, though most of the young people speak Thai well. Many of the Karen people are Christian in the Mae Hong Son province, in North Thailand.

According to Sandra, the Karen people are extremely calm, easygoing people. The women are treated as equal to men. Generally the Karen people are less materialistic, and drink less alcohol than Thais (who tend to look down on them). Also Karen communities are run democratically, though the village heads and elders, who make the decisions, are male.

The Karen men are generally monogamous; polygamy is frowned upon. Usually Karen couples are not expected to support their families financially, though they always take care of their parents; they have no expectations of *farang* women.

In the Karen marriage ceremony, the ceremonial blessing, which lasts two days, does not involve any exchange of vows. First there is a ceremony at the bride's village and then another in the husband's village. The couple are blessed while guests drink locally brewed rice wine (*laokhaw*). Pigs are slaughtered to ward off evil spirits.

Close family members eat together first, and later the other villagers join them. Each of the guests tie string around the couples' wrists; the strands should remain on them for up to a week. There is no dowry system existing in Karen tribes. Wedding gifts usually include money and clothes, as well as silver and bronze bracelets.

## SUMMARY

- In Thailand, the ultimate destination for female *farang* sex tourists is Haad Rin, in Koh Pha Ngan, where there are regular full- and half-moon Parties to bring them into contact with the Thai beach boys';
- A growing number of foreign women have committed relationships with men from Thailand's hill tribes.

# THE REAL COST OF LOVE

*Instead of getting married again, I'm going to find a woman I
don't like and give her a house*

Rod Stewart,

*Purchase a piece of property, and get a woman as part of the deal*

Boaz (Ruth 4:5-10)

Every foreign man who wants a long-term commitment from a Thai
lady should expect to pay for the privilege. What a Thai spouse
expects from her partner depends on her family circumstances, social
status, education and what her friends say. Southeast Asians are
strongly influenced by their friends and family.

If you are thinking about committing to a relationship with
a Thai girl it is necessary to treat the process as though it were a
formal business transaction, particularly in the early stages. This is
unromantic business, but necessary. Before the emotional heart strings
come into play, it is necessary to structure a mutually beneficial and
equitable deal between the two of you.

Think about what an astute businessman would do when
considering the purchase of an investment. He would request a full
background history from the owner and set about validating the

information (through due diligence). If he were to find any of the representations to be false, he would not pursue the opportunity. Background checking of a spouse-to-be is covered in the chapter entitled: 'The Love Audit'.

Once the good businessman has checked that the other businessperson's representations are correct, he would negotiate a price for the investment. He would involve a lawyer and other impartial professionals. He would not be emotionally involved in the transaction. He would consider every potential pitfall and create ways of limiting the risk of each. Negotiating a fair deal in exchange for your Thai bride is covered in this chapter. Protecting your Thailand-based assets is covered in the chapter: 'Protect your Assets!'

The adept businessman also knows who to negotiate with. A common mistake is to spend hours negotiating with a person who does not have the authority to ratify the deal. Negotiate with the real decision makers. If you want to negotiate marriage with a Thai lady, the decision makers are usually her parents.

Divorce in cross-culture marriages is least likely with Filipino ladies. According to the Institute of National Statistics, nintey-seven and a half percent of Filipino–Western couples are still married after two years, compared to eighty percent for Thai–*farang* marriages.

Beware that your partner's response and her parents' response may not meld as closely as you would like. She will probably tell you want you want to hear, and that's not necessarily the truth.

## NEGOTIATIONS

### Chaperones

It is still common in Thailand for men to date a respectable lady in the presence of chaperones, who are usually trusted friends or family members. The lady will continue to be chaperoned until they are convinced of the man's respectability and his commitment to the relationship. This process may endure for weeks, months or even years.

## Mediation

Many *farang* husbands extol the benefits of using a third-party mediator (*porsoo*) to help with the negotiation process. The mediator is your bridge to your partner's parents. Their job, as agent, is to act on your behalf, towards establishing an equitable relationship contract for all parties concerned.

The mediator must be a Thai person who carries social status (for example a government official, lawyer or doctor) and authority. You must trust your mediator to tell you everything. Of course your mediator needs to be able to communicate clearly with both you and your partner's parents.

Part of the mediator's role is to promote you as their daughter's ideal husband. This may mean highlighting your career achievements and any evidence of good character.

## Decisions

There is a lot more to the negotiation process than agreeing a price for the dowry (or *sin sot*). Other considerations which need to be discussed are:
- The monthly allowance to pay your partner;
- A monthly stipend for your partner's parents;
- Provision of a home and land;
- Gifting of gold (or *thong mun*);

- The date of the wedding (on an auspicious day);
- The wedding ceremony arrangements.

According to Nikki Assavathorn, the bride's family is responsible for the cost of the marriage ceremony, subject to the following caveat: 'The amount the bride paid towards the ceremony should be matched by the groom and be given to the bride's family'. Usually the costs of the wedding ceremony are financed by part of the dowry.

### The Decision Makers

Find out who are the main decision makers. Usually the people who make the decisions are your partner's parents but check whether there are any other significant influencers. Pitch your case to all the main decision makers. A salesman's worst nightmare is hearing the following words after a long sales presentation 'I will let you know after I have spoken to my boss'.

An important part of the decision-making process for Thai people is positive validation of the union by a respected fortune-teller (*mor doo*). Bill, who is from Los Angeles, introduced his spouse's family to his fortune-teller, a good friend of his, because he didn't want to leave his destiny to chance. Of course he gave his friend a bottle of whisky for his positive commendation.

## THE MARRIAGE PROCESS

### Engagement

The main purpose of engagement is for the couple to formally introduce each other to their respective families and to confirm the terms of the marriage (including the dowry) and the date of the wedding.

Usually gold jewellery (*thong mun*) is presented to the lady at a betrothal ceremony, known as *phitee mun*, at her parent's home. This ceremony is attended by a select group of family and friends. The groom is introduced to her family by a friend, and gifts are presented to her family.

After the man promises to take care of his partner, and her family agrees, the couple are '*koo mun*', which means 'tied together' or engaged. Afterwards a meal is served. Sometime afterwards or on the same day, there will be an actual wedding ceremony.

## The Buddhist Wedding Ceremony

At a traditional Buddhist wedding ceremony there should be an odd number of monks present, usually five, seven or nine, to perform the rituals. Odd numbers are considered sacred, and the number nine is deemed to be especially lucky. The monks always face the west.

The most senior monk chants in the ancient Pali language to initiate the ceremony and bestow blessings on the bride and groom; and they kneel on the ground next to each other in front of the monks, holding their hands in the traditional *wai* position to signify respect.

The senior monk drapes a symbolic thread around the couple to signify commitment to one another. The monk also sprinkles holy water on the newlyweds using a leafy twig or sea shell 'so they will live longer'. The couple gives small presents and donations (typically 200 baht each) to the monks before further prayers. The ceremony usually lasts less than an hour.

During the *bai sri soo kwan* ceremony, each guest ties string around the wrist of the bride and the groom whilst blessing the newlyweds. Finally they place garlands of flowers around both the bride and groom. The day after the wedding, the newlyweds usually visit their parents to pay their respects with gifts.

The Buddhist wedding ceremony authenticates your partnership socially and spiritually but not legally.

## Legal Marriage in Thailand

Getting legally married in Thailand is usually a quick and easy process. The marriage is recognized overseas if it is valid according to Thai law (by registration at an *amphur* office in Thailand).

To be eligible for marriage in Thailand, both people: a) must be over seventeen years of age (otherwise consent to the marriage is required by an underage person's parents); b) cannot be directly related; c) must not be already married; d) cannot marry their own adopted child (as Woody Allen did); e) cannot remarry until 310 days after the date of divorce or death of their previous spouse (unless the couple has a child).

Marriages can be registered at any *amphur* office in Thailand (on working days between 8.00am and 3.00pm). You need to provide your passport and evidence that you are not married. Your Thai partner must provide her ID card and *tabian baan* (evidence of registered home) as well as the names and addresses of two people who live in the same district. The marriage must be witnessed by two people.

You must sign an affirmation (or affidavit) of Freedom to Marry (FTM) and get it notarized by your embassy in Bangkok. These forms are supplied by your country's embassy in Bangkok. For a list of embassies, refer to the website: *http://www.embassyworld.com.* The FTM must be translated into Thai by an accredited translator (or lawyer) before submitting it to the Ministry of Foreign Affairs

(Department of Consular Affairs) in Bangkok for approval. The approved FTM is valid for ninety days.

The FTM document is available for download at the Ministry of Foreign Affairs' website: *http://www.mfa.go.th/web/150.php*. The Department of Consular Affairs at the Ministry of Foreign Affairs is located at the following address:

The Ministry of Foreign Affairs
123 Chaeng Wattana Road
Laksi District
Bangkok 11120
Telephone: +66 (0)2 575-1056/59
Email: consular04@mfa.go.th
Internet: http://www.mfa.go.th
Office hours: 0.830 – 11.30 and 13.00 – 15.30

If you are a divorcee, you will need to provide the original divorce certificate. If your previous spouse died, you must provide the original death certificate. Otherwise, you must sign a declaration stating that you have never been married.

The *amphur* office usually takes less than thirty minutes to register a marriage. The officer provides two marriage certificates written in Thai.

It is not usually possible to register Thailand-registered marriages outside the Land of Smiles. However, some countries, including the United Kingdom, allow Thai marriage certificates to be translated into English and deposited with the British General Registry Office.

### Legal Marriage outside Thailand

If you marry a Thai lady outside Thailand she will still be considered single according to Thai law unless the marriage is registered at a Thai embassy or consulate. Many Thai ladies prefer to get married outside Thailand so they can keep their legal status of being a single person in Thailand.

## THE PRICE OF LOVE

The main upfront costs of marrying a Thai lady are gold, dowry (known as *sin sot*) and the marriage ceremony. The Thai word *sin* means 'riches' and *sot* means 'saving'. It is normal for the groom to provide a house as well. It is usually necessary to provide continuous financial support to the wife and her family; this varies according to their social status and economic circumstances.

### The Dowry (*Sin Sot*)

In Thailand a dowry is usually payable to the bride's parents. Thais believe that a prospective husband owes his fiancé's parents for bringing up the daughter to be a decent lady and wife. A quainter way to view the dowry is the mother's 'milk money' (*kar nam nom*) which literally means the money she owes for her mother's breast milk, rather like the future husband repaying her family for her upbringing. The dowry is compensation for the family's loss of labour (and wealth) resulting from the marriage. The dowry is also a symbolic demonstration of the groom's financial ability to support a family.

By contrast, in India, the wife's family pays a dowry to her husband in exchange for the promise that he will support her financially during the marriage. In Thailand the husband is usually expected to pay both ways: via the dowry down-payment and future financial support to his wife and her family.

The value of Thai dowry depends upon the woman's social status, beauty, age and eligibility, education and whether she is a virgin. Usually the dowry amount is considerably less if the lady was previously married or if she has children. The asking price tends to be higher when the groom is foreign or if the lady's parents are financially insecure.

At least ten percent of Thai marriages proceed without any transfer of sin sot, and the number is growing. Many Thai brides have reasonable parents who are willing to return all or part of the dowry after the wedding ceremony.

The value of a dowry varies between US$1,000 and over US$300,000. A woman from northeast Thailand would typically command between US$1,500 and US$3,000. A middle-class woman would normally be valued at between US$3,000 and US$15,000. And a woman from an affluent family would expect well over US$20,000. Film actresses and pop stars are at the top end, from US$250,000.

In November 2007, Prem Busarakhamwong offered pop singer Tata Young a dowry worth 100 million baht (US$3 million). The gifts included a 5.5-carat diamond ring and a silk-lined box filled with eighteen gold bars.

Bob from California paid a US$1,600 dowry and three-dollar measures of gold. His spouse's parents initially asked for US$2,250. He negotiated a down-payment of US$300 with the balance payable over twelve months, interest free.

According to Bob, 'It's important to have a display of money at the wedding, usually in US$100 notes because it looks like there is more money and it stops others from counting it. This symbolic gesture demonstrates your intention to take care of your wife. It's also a face-saver for her family, and often they will return the display money to you after the ceremony if it is not part of the dowry'.

The Thai Professional introduction agency recommends their clients pay a dowry of around US$2,000. Just Thai Ladies suggest a dowry of around US$3,000 and charge an administration fee of ten percent on all funds remitted through their payment gateway.

The contract (involving the dowry) is between the lady's family and the husband-to-be. The agent acts as a mediator but an agent usually has a vested interest in acting on behalf of the Thai fiancé. Most agencies receive a 'bonus' from the Thai lady's family after the dowry has been paid (but this usually denied by the parties concerned). For more details, refer to the chapter: 'Agents of Love'.

Remember that many families do not insist upon any dowry nowadays, and some return all of part of the money after the wedding ceremony. The key to a mutually agreeable marriage 'deal' is open clear communication, patience, negotiation and a willingness to compromise.

Don't expect to receive a refund of the dowry if the marriage ends in divorce. Occasionally Thai men manage to recover their dowry monies after they discovered their wives' infidelity. Most foreigners would be expected to write off the dowry as a lesson in cross-cultural relations.

---

### Case Study

A Thai man employed by the Army paid his Thai wife's family in Khon Kaen a dowry of 150,000 baht (US$4,500) and gave

---

> her gold weighing 152 grams (or ten baht by weight). The wife
> worked as a secretary on a salary of US$150 per month. Some
> *farang* give similar amounts to the families of their wives in
> Northeast Thailand.

### Thong Mun

In Thailand most couples get engaged in a traditional ceremony
known as *thong mun*, which literally means 'gold engagement'.
During this ceremony, which is attended by close family and friends,
the prospective bridegroom gives gold to his fiancé.

The weight of the gold jewellery—which is twenty-four carat—
should be at least two baht by weight (or 30.4 grams) for the
ceremony; giving less would be considered mean (*kii niow*) and bad
luck for the relationship. Gold weighing two baht costs over US$700.
Gifting gold in an even number of baht by weight—typically two,
four, six or eight—is deemed auspicious for the marriage.

Typically the bridegroom gives between two and ten baht weight
of gold to his fiancé—average five-baht weight—according to his
affluence and generosity.

Many Thai couples live together in common law marriages,
without registering their relationship at any municipal (*amphur*)
office. Many Thai ladies believe that the gift of gold says much more
about the status of the relationship than any marriage certificate.

### Support for the Spouse and Family

Most Thai ladies expect to stop working after getting married to a
*farang* man. If they continue to work, all their friends and family
would remind her of Thai wives they know who don't have to work.

She would lose face and the family would wonder whether she is married to a stingy man.

It is usual for foreign husbands to pay their spouse a monthly allowance as compensation for their lost earnings when they terminate their employment. Many foreigners in Northern Thailand pay their spouses an allowance of at least US$300 each month. It is not unusual for them to also pay around US$200 each month to the spouse's family.

## The Home

Foreigners are not allowed to own land in Thailand but most Thai families own their own land. Most foreigners finance the building of a marital home on their spouse's land. If you are lucky, your spouse will bring land into the matrimonial deal.

The actual cost of building a home depends on the size, quality of workmanship, location and materials used. However, as a guide, a standard three bedroom home outside a city may cost up to US$35,000 to build.

Your Thai spouse is allowed to buy land and property in Thailand. Improvements to the property, such as a house, can be legally owned by *farang*; whereas the land on which it is built cannot.

For ways of protecting your property investments in Thailand, refer to the chapter, 'Protect your Assets!'

## Children

If your partner does not have any children and she is under the age of thirty-five, she probably wants to have children. Most Thai families rely on their offspring for support during retirement because their social security system is family and community oriented. Therefore your financial plans should include provision for your children.

## SECRETS TO A HAPPY MARRIAGE

A happy cross-culture marriage requires clear communication, a secure economy, good family relations and a healthy dose of delusion.

### Clear Communication

The happiest cross-culture relationships are based upon an equitable, mutually agreed, relationship contract. The terms of the relationship are openly discussed, negotiated and agreed; and periodically evaluated. Relationship contracts are explained in the chapter entitled 'Love Contracts'.

### Secure Economy

Most marriage breakups arise due to economic problems, according to cross-culture relationship consultant, Vanessa Tan. If your Asian spouse and her family are adequately secure financially the risk of broken hearts are reduced considerably.

### Good Family Relations

When you marry a Thai lady, it is essential that you get on well with your spouse's family. A Thai lady's primary responsibility is towards her parents and family, then her husband. If you cannot relate positively with your Thai partner's parents, the relationship will probably not succeed.

## Healthy Delusion

Delusion is the secret to successful marriage according to Tyler Cohen in his book *Discover your Inner Economist*. Psychologists refer to such unrealistic and exaggerated positive assessment of one's spouse as 'marital aggrandizement'. In Asia it can be turned around to show that many spouses are in denial of their partner's negative attributes, particularly their philandering behavior.

Many married couples admit that they lost interest in their sex life after tying the knot. But the delusion remains: Most Asians believe their sex life is better than average. Tyler Cohen reports that seventeen percent of married couples admit to not having sex with their spouse during the previous month. The question is: How many of the remaining eighty-three percent were lying?

# ... AND FINALLY

## Be Prepared

Sure, it's extremely unromantic to ask your fiancé to sign a prenuptial agreement before you get married, but doing so may save you a lot of money and grief. Be warned that many Thai women get extremely upset when asked to sign prenuptial agreements. Typically they say 'That means you don't trust me! OK, let's finish!' Don't back down, or she will control you completely forever.

Keep ahead of the game: If you want to insure against divorce, don't get married—or ensure you both commit to your relationship contract. For guidance about negotiating workable cross-culture relationship deals, refer to the chapter 'Love Contracts'.

**Divorce**

If you want to annul your legal relationship contract with your Thai spouse, and render it null and void, you must apply for a divorce. But before you rush off to your lawyer's office, consider the alternatives of relationship counseling, mediation or even a trial separation. Perhaps you have more things to teach each other.

Divorce in Thailand can be obtained by mutual consent in writing. The affirmation must be witnessed by two people and registered at a local *amphur* office. The *amphur* office will issue a divorce certificate upon registration. It is not necessary to instruct a lawyer if both spouses consent to the divorce.

The following documents should support the application: your passport, your spouse's national identity card, household registration (*tabian baan*) and original marriage certificate.

A Thai lady is allowed to readopt her maiden name immediately after the divorce.

If mutual consent to divorce is not possible, then an application should be presented to the Thai family court for legal judgment. This route can be expensive because it will be necessary to instruct a Thai lawyer who will typically ask for an initial deposit of US$30,000 prior to litigation.

Acceptable grounds for divorce in Thailand include gross misconduct, causing physical or emotional injury; insanity; adultery; desertion for more than twelve months; legal imprisonment for more than one year; disappearance or change of domicile; lack of maintenance or financial support; one partner having an incurable contagious disease; three years of separation; physical incapacity, including impotence.

If you are living outside Thailand, and you and your wife got married in Thailand, then the divorce must also take place in Thailand too. If your Thai wife contests the divorce, then it is necessary to apply to the law court in Thailand. Although a Thai lawyer may act on your behalf during the preliminary stages of divorce (subject to a valid power of attorney), you must appear in court for the final judgment.

In 'Farangland' divorces can be traumatic affairs. Author Barry Sandal summarizes his experience: 'In [the West], the woman wants to cut off our balls, take everything and ensure that the children hate us. Then the court whips us into submission, processes us and siphons our money from the bank to pay alimony and child support. The legal system works for her, and it really humiliates and humbles a man terribly.'

Divorces are much more reasonable in Thailand. Land and property is relatively cheap, so, according to Barry Sandal, 'The man says "You take the house and the kids; I will still be the father, but now you are wife number two." It's all very tame compared to the West.'

## SUMMARY

- A dowry (known as *sin sot*) is usually payable by the man to the fiancé's family;
- The price of the dowry, which needs to be negotiated, is influenced by the social status and affluence of the lady's family;
- It is usual to use a mediator, or trusted friend, to negotiate with the lady's parents on behalf of the man;
- A marriage registered at an *amphur* office in Thailand

is legally recognized overseas; however if you marry a
Thai lady overseas, she will still have the legal rights
of a single person in Thailand;

- The marital relationship is unlikely to survive if you
cannot get along well with your wife's family;

- In Thailand 'true love usually comes later', after the man
has already demonstrated his commitment to the
relationship;

- Treat the cross-culture relationship as a business deal,
particularly in the early stages of negotiations.

# AGENTS OF LOVE

*Can I borrow US$750 to see me through until I meet my* farang
*husband-to-be?*

A Thai lady member of a Chiang Mai introduction agency

Introduction agencies are another group of Love Entrepreneurs that benefit from cross-culture relationships (and vise versa). These relationship intermediaries provide a match-making service in return for a fee.

Many of the introduction agencies in Thailand serve foreigners who are looking for a spouse to live with them in their Western home. Typically these agencies arrange a few face-to-face meetings with suitable candidates while the foreigner is in Thailand on vacation.

Introduction agencies work on behalf of the Thai lady, just as a real estate agent works on behalf of the property owner. The introduction agent's job is to market the Thai ladies to the *farang* men. The men pay for the service, although the ladies usually pay a nominal registration fee to join the agency.

Most introduction agencies tell their foreign clients that they receive no fee out of the dowry. However, the reality is sometimes different. One Thai lady was forced to sell her gold engagement ring to pay commission to her introduction agency (amounting to fifty percent of the dowry received).

Many introduction agencies also earn fees from visa consulting. Some of the agents offer a professional service, while others bluff their way through the process. For more information about fiancé and marriage visas, refer to the chapter 'Relationship Visas'.

The main difference between introduction agencies and online dating systems is quality control of the members. Online dating systems can only guarantee that their members have an email address. Introduction agencies usually provide some background checks on their members.

Usually the *farang* members pay more than the local Asian members. One introduction agency in the north of Thailand charges foreign men five times what they charge local women.

Research a few introduction agencies before you select one. Ask for references from satisfied clients; see if you can talk to one of the agency's clients who have been through the whole process.

In many parts of Asia it is customary for businesses, including brokers, to receive commissions from affiliated businesses whenever business is referred to them. Introduction agencies benefit from myriad potential referral commissions (or kickbacks) from hotels, car hire companies, taxi services, tour operators, wedding gown suppliers, real estate agents, jewellers, florists and so on. The commissions vary from ten percent to fifty percent (for highly competitive services, such as luxury spa treatments).

In this section, three completely different introduction agencies are profiled. The first agency, called MeetNLunch, is for educated English-speaking professional Thais and *farang* living in the Bangkok area. The second is an agency based in Northern Thailand, called Just Thai Ladies, which is a full-service marriage agency for Thai ladies wanting to live overseas. The third agency is an unidentified 'hobby business' run by a Thai–*farang* couple.

## MEETNLUNCH

The co-founder and director of MeetNLunch (MNL), Khun Nikki Assavathorn, regularly contributes articles about dating to the *Bangkok Post*'s *Guru Magazine*.

Nikki was educated at a British boarding school before studying chemistry at Imperial College London. Nikki currently works as an energy consultant while managing MNL.

The three hundred- to four hundred-strong membership of MNL comprises professional, educated Thais and foreign expats. This is the number of single people at any one time who are available for dating. According to MNL's website, seventy percent of the membership is Thai. The agency enrolls twenty new members every week.

Approximately half of Nikki's registered men are *farang* expats, residing in or near Bangkok. MNL's expatriate members are mainly business people, though some have teaching jobs and others are wealthy semi-retired. Most of the registered men, aged twenty-seven to fifty-two, are looking for attractive, educated Thai ladies.

Sixty percent of the agency's membership is female. The female members, aged twenty-four upwards, often have professional careers, and some want to meet foreign men and live overseas.

Most of the female members are Thai, though there are some *farang* members. There is lesser demand for foreign women because they are perceived as less feminine than their Thai sisters. Most *farang* men are specifically looking for petite Asian ladies, and the professional Thai men are usually turned off by strong-minded *farang* women with larger physical builds than themselves.

MNL have stringent joining criteria. All members must have regular income, speak English and be single residents in Thailand. Tourists and short-term visitors are not eligible for this social networking club, which is integrated into the Bangkok Young Professional (BYP) scene. MNL's low key approach is similar to the Singapore-based agency, Lunch Actually. The American matchmaking franchise It's Just Lunch has offices in both Singapore and Bangkok (*http://www.itsjustlunchbangkok.com*).

Thai male members of MNL typically have professional careers and their own (or family) businesses. MNL enables professional Thais to integrate with professional expats. This service suits busy professional people who like delegating organizational tasks.

MNL charges in the region of US$180 (6,000 baht) for three qualified appointments. MNL customer services book a table at a suitable restaurant.

## How It Works

*Step 1 Interview:* The initial step is a meeting with Nikki in Bangkok. The purpose of this one hour meeting is for Nikki to get to know her client and the specifications of their ideal partner. Also the client gets the opportunity to learn how the introduction service works.

Prior to the meeting, the client receives a brief email from MNL Customer Care, asking him or her to bring a copy of their passport (or ID card) to the meeting.

The meetings are usually held at a coffee shop in Siam Paragon. Nikki charges US$30 for the initial consultation (including the cost of any drinks ordered); but she does not charge for the meeting if she has nobody to match you with.

Before closing the meeting, Nikki asks the client to sign a copy of the agency's Terms and Conditions. The small print covers non-competition policy and breach of conduct for inappropriate behavior, or by providing the agency with false information about marital status.

*Step 2 Lunch dates:* Next, the agency conducts a database search of prospective partners and arranges some lunchtime or dinner meetings. Nikki uses the information provided in conjunction with her intuition. These meetings are arranged in selective public places. Bacchus wine bar and restaurant at Ruam Rudee Village is one of MNL's meeting places.

The client is asked to deposit the agency fee into MNL's bank account. The dates are arranged and the arrangements are emailed to the clients. The mobile phone number of the date is sent by text message.

*Step 3 Feedback:* Members are asked to feed back their experiences to Nikki after each lunch date. This information enables the agency to refine the database information and update the candidate's specification.

---

### Case Study # 1

The purpose of this case study is to demonstrate the type of member you are likely to meet through MeetNLunch.

One of the dates was called Air, an attractive thirty-four-year-old Thai lady who is fluent in English and works as a university lecturer in Bangkok. She has a master's degree from

---

America, thanks to some financial help from her parents. She later received a scholarship from the Thai government to study for a PhD in linguistics in England.

Air explained that she is tied to employment with the Thai government for nine years, twice the duration of her scholarship overseas. If she breaks her contract she has to pay three times the cost of the scholarship, in the region of US$250,000. Air is really tied to Thailand for a long time.

Air had recently broken up with her British fiancé. She said her plans of having a family evaporated last year on the date of the breakup. She is exceptionally attached to planning for her future.

Her fiancé was scared off by her controlling parents who demanded that the couple live together with them. Air explained how socially aware her parents are; they continually warn her 'People are watching you, you know!' When asked whether she would consider having another Thai boyfriend she answered 'Never. I would prefer to be single.'

When asked about living in the UK, Air said she enjoyed the experience and liked the people there. However, she thought that the British weather was bad for her health and the high-calorie diet made her gain weight. Air says that the *farang* living in Thailand are much more interesting than the ones in the UK.

After one and a half hours, she politely left to 'powder her nose' and report her progress to her best friend. This procedure appeared to be a security measure to protect her safety. Air mentioned she had 'backup plans' in case her date is a psychotic maniac.

Air is nice and like many Thai ladies, she is highly influenced by her parents. Westerners might view such influence as immature but really it is strong cultural conditioning. Thai ladies are duty-bound to please their parents.

### Case Study # 2

The second lady is also very attractive, polite and educated to degree level. She has her own business and is financially independent. She neither drinks alcohol nor smokes. She even nursed her parents throughout their declining years. In many ways she would be the perfect partner.

Most of the checkboxes of the 'match criteria' were ticked, but there was something lacking: the Wow! factor, which many guys yearn for. It's often this factor which brings risk into the relationship—as well as a lot of fun. Naughtiness in moderation is a blessing; but too much of it is a recipe for the perfect brief encounter.

There are some extremely attractive professional Thai ladies with good personalities registered with MeetNLunch. Any expat living near Bangkok who is seeking friendship or a serious relationship with an educated Thai lady should consider this service.

For further information about MeetNLunch, refer to the website: *http://www.meetnlunch.com.*

For a list of accredited matchmakers in Asia, refer to the Matchmaking Institute website: *http://www.matchmakinginstitute.com.*

# JUST THAI LADIES

Just Thai Ladies (JTL) is a full-service introduction agency based in Chiang Rai for marriage-minded foreigners and Thai ladies who want to live outside Thailand. The agency is run by a Briton and his Thai wife. The JTL agency, formerly owned by Paul (an Australian) and his Thai wife, Nee, was profiled before it was taken over by its current management.

Paul emphasizes that JTL is not an escort agency. Paul once received a phone call from a foreign man asking 'Can you send over a girl to my hotel room at 9pm?' JTL is not that kind of agency.

Love Entrepreneur Paul believes that foreign men who can offer financial security and loyalty to sincere Thai wives will be reciprocated fivefold by way of tender loving care.

## Validating Members

Nee checks the personal identity of each female member and confirms their residential address against their house registration book. JTL is associated with a local private investigation bureau which can check the woman's marital status, police records and whether she has any children. Occasionally Thai ladies conceal the fact they have husbands or children. For further information about background checks, refer to the chapter, 'The Love Audit'.

AIDS tests can be arranged for both parties at Chiang Mai Ram Hospital. Some men, who want their lady to be tested, are reluctant to take the test themselves. 'Why should I need to take the test?' they ask. Paul retorts, 'So why is it so important for the lady to take the test?' Paul and Nee demand respect for their lady members.

Nee asks her lady members to provide their employment details.

She phones their employer to confirm the information is correct. Some of the ladies who apply for membership of JTL are already married or have Thai boyfriends. Paul opens a drawer containing application forms of about 150 blacklisted members who failed to meet their membership criteria.

Only one lady out of JTL's 300 registered female members smokes cigarettes. Respectable Thai ladies do not usually smoke cigarettes, sport tattoos or wear immodest clothing.

Some of the lady members do not speak English so JTL provide a translation service and also arrange English lessons for them.

**How It Works**

A prospective male candidate, who is either working or retired, will register with JTL in cyberspace at *http://www.justthailadies.com*. Typically, he will visit JTL in Northern Thailand during a vacation and meet up to five Thai ladies. Once an appropriate match is made, negotiations begin.

Some foreign men opt for the correspondence-based membership initially. Most of the registered Thai ladies speak and write poor English, so translation and interpretation are important aspects of JTL's service. Thai ladies who speak English fluently need careful vetting because they may have worked in the bars or had previous relationships with foreigners.

The average dowry, which is paid by the man to the bride's family, is 100,000 baht (US$3,000). It is common for the family to request a higher amount with a promise to return part of the money to the bridegroom after the wedding. A large dowry commands social status in the local community, whereas a small dowry may cause loss of face to the bride's family.

Sometimes relationships break up due to the reluctance or inability of the man to pay for a dowry. One wealthy male client, who had money tied up in investments, was unable to pay a large dowry initially. Shortly after the lady rejected her suitor, her bank issued her with a foreclosure notice, so she lost her home as well.

Usually the man offers to pay the lady a monthly allowance to enable her to give up her employment and offer some support to her family. Typically, male members transfer 10,000 baht (US$300) each month to JTL who distribute the money to the respective female members' bank accounts. JTL charge a 10% administration fee on all funds remitted to their agency.

One of JTL's male members, who had an issue about trusting Thai ladies, asked to interview the ladies under polygraph (lie detector). He was a fifty-seven-year-old American who wanted to marry a twenty-three-year-old Thai lady and finance her medical training in USA. She was his 'health insurance policy' for his remaining years of old age.

Initially, JTL advises lady members to apply for tourist visas when visiting their partner's country of residence. Later they can apply for fiancé visas if they intend to marry within three to nine months of arrival. The visa application process takes at least ten weeks longer if the couple is already married (due to additional administration).

### What Thai Ladies Really Want

According to Paul and Nee, most Thai ladies want security and a monogamous relationship. Many Thai ladies complain about their previous Thai husband's infidelity and most struggle to support themselves and their children on a monthly salary of around US$200. Nearly all sincere Thai ladies look after their husbands well if they are provided financial security by a faithful husband. In Thailand there is no law requiring child support payments from fathers, and just a few men voluntarily contribute to their broken families.

A brief review of the lady members on the JTL website reveals that most of the ladies want a more mature husband, usually in the age range forty to sixty years old. These women, who are keen to settle down, value a secure home, a large nest egg and a faithful man to look after.

Most of the ladies registered with JTL are sincere. However one cheeky female member asked Nee for a US$750 loan which she promised to repay as soon as she met her foreign husband. A common complaint amongst foreign men is that Thai ladies treat them like mobile ATMs which dispense a bottomless pile of banknotes.

Paul and Nee are consulted by their members on personal issues too. One member asked for advice about erectile dysfunction. Paul and Nee referred the client to a local consultant who specialized in this particular health issue.

For further information about Just Thai Ladies, visit their website at: *http://www.justthailadies.com.*

## VISA ASSISTANCE

The following comments were posted on the Thaivisa.com discussion forums:

> 'Beware agencies who say that they can guarantee a visa for your partner, they are lying.'

> 'If you do meet your partner through an agency, do not worry about telling the embassy this on any subsequent visa application. As long as the relationship is genuine the

embassy does not really care how you met each other. Some agencies will tell you different, and encourage you to make things up for the visa application. Don't listen to them!'

'I have heard of at least one agency that demanded more money from a couple they had introduced in order to 'help' them prepare their visa application. When they refused the agency told them that they stood no chance of getting a visa without their help; which is rubbish.'

## CUTE THAI LADIES

There are several freelance introduction agents throughout Thailand. Usually these agencies are Thai–*farang* couples who are running a small business on a shoestring budget. Cute Thai Ladies (CTL), which has been renamed, is one such example of a 'hobby business' managed by a couple of Love Entrepreneurs, Nok and Jimmy.

The *Chiangmai Mail* listed an introduction agency for sale in its online classified section. The business was described as 'profitable', 'established' and 'a bargain for 30,000 baht (US$900)'. This business sounded like a good source of research material about Love Entrepreneurs, so it was investigated.

The British guy who answered the telephone enquiry had a Brummie accent, like Jasper Carrott. When asked about the introduction agency advertised for sale in the local newspaper, he replied 'Oh, that! My girlfriend was having a bad day when she placed that ad; so it's not really for sale!' When asked whether the agency might still be available at an appropriate price, the reply was: 'Sure! When do you want to meet?' I asked what the current selling price of the agency was, and was told 100,000 baht (or US$3,000) after some background whispering.

I met Jimmy and his Thai girlfriend in a local Chiang Mai hotel. Jimmy explained that the cost of developing the CTL website alone was US$900. He explained that many introduction agencies simply sell the website template, and allow other businesses to startup using a different name. He seemed to be inviting me to make an offer of US$900 for the CTL website design (without the inventory of attractive ladies, but with a few hours of induction training over a Chiang beer).

Obviously most of the 200 registered members are Thai ladies, but there are between ten and twenty registered *farang* members. The ladies pay a US$6 registration fee. Men are supposed to buy flowers for the lady (at a cost of US$30) each time they correspond with her. CTL's cost of buying the flowers and delivering them to the lady is under US$5.

Jimmy explains that helping customers with their visa applications is a really good earner for the agency. 'We can charge as much as 30,000 baht (US$900) for processing a customer's fiancé visa.' Says Nok. 'That's what you were asking for your business on your bad day!' I replied.

Jimmy says that the ladies nearly always pay them a generous 'bonus' of at least 50,000 baht (US$1,500) when the couple gets married. This money is part of the dowry (*sin sot*), which the man pays to the bride's family. Jimmy says that most agencies deny receiving any 'bonus' out of the dowry, but it's actually common practice throughout Asia.

Another source of income for the agency comes from translation of written correspondence at US$6 per page. So there are several ways for Love Entrepreneurs in this line of business to earn money.

## OTHER AGENCIES

There are several other introduction agencies in Thailand which charge fees in the range US$1,500 to US$5,000. These intermediaries include Family Thai, Thai Wives, Thai Professional and Siam Introductions.

Thai Darling is another introduction service which arranges personal meetings in exchange for a monthly fee. Thai Darling's website is: *http://www.thaidarling.com.*

The Sweet Singles introduction agency boasts a female membership of over 4,000. The address of the Sweet Singles website is: *http://www.sweetsingles.com.* They have three classifications of female member: Special Lady, Sweet Lady and Trial Lady.

## SUMMARY

- There are two main types of introduction agencies in Thailand: marriage agencies for couples wanting to live in farangland, and local introduction services for Thais and expats.

- Introduction agencies usually qualify their registered members by validating each application. There is usually some degree of quality control; conversely, online dating services just guarantee that members have their own email address.

- Don't feel coy about telling your embassy that you met your Thai fiancé at an introduction agency. All they want to know is whether your relationship is genuine or not.

# OPPORTUNITIES IN THE FOOD & BEVERAGE INDUSTRY

*You can take the girl from the bar, but you can't take the bar from the girl.*

**A WISE GUY**

Many of Thailand's 11.5 million annual visitors arrive in the Land of Smiles for entertainment: golf, water sports, health spas and raunchy nightlife. Some guys find themselves smitten with bargirls (girls who work in local bars and restaurants) and later get confused about their relationship. Many of these beautiful and enchanting ladies working in bars and restaurants are available. This chapter offers guidance for anyone wanting to consort with these alluring Love Entrepreneurs.

## FACT 1: BARGIRLS ARE PAID TO LIE

Sex workers are actresses and purveyors of illusion. Many bargirls use a pseudonym such as 'Go' or 'Bunny' to demarcate their personal life from their professional life. The top earners enable even the saddest obese old man to feel like David Beckham. The tools of their trade are charm, flattery, seduction and playful mind games.

It is generally acknowledged that bargirls are economical with the truth. Many of their stories are typecast clichés designed to attract sympathy and generosity. Their remit is to create illusions. Deception is a key aspect of their job spec. Therefore, to ascertain the truth, it is necessary to compare the bargirl's 'story' with other peoples' accounts of the same story.

Nee is from Thailand's depressed northeast province of Issan. She says she is forty-one years old and that she started working as a bargirl twelve months ago. Her father, who was an alcoholic electrician, died of cancer ten years earlier. She believes she would not have to work in the bars if her father was still alive. She says her only daughter lives with her mother in Sansai.

After three months working at the bar she met a rich German called Hans who works for Mercedes Benz in Stuttgart. They spent four weeks together on Koh Pha Ngan island enjoying a hot romance in paradise.

Nee and Hans planned a life together in Germany, and Hans agreed to help her apply for a fiancé visa. He also agreed to send her a monthly allowance of 40,000 baht (US$1,200) to enable her to stop working at the bar. Some months Hans sent 50,000 or 60,000 baht to meet Nees's requests to cover 'additional expenses'.

Nee says that Hans stopped paying her monthly allowance after seven months. At the same time he broke off all communication with her. Hans would not accept her phone calls or reply to her emails or letters. Nee claims she does not understand the reason for his change of heart. 'Maybe he has a new girlfriend?' she suggests.

Nee returned to work at the bar three weeks after the meltdown of her relationship with Hans. So it was back to 'business as usual' after seven months off work. She says she never wants to marry again because her heart is broken. She cannot trust *farang* men ever again. Recently she began seeing a Finnish man but she thinks he too will forget her quickly.

Nee claims she is good at her job, but 'it is not good for my heart'. She enjoys drinking copious quantities of beer so she carries an additional twenty-five kilograms since last year. Forty-one years of age is old for this type of work because it is the twenty-year-old vixens who attract most customers. Nee says she plans to work as a bargirl for another five years before starting her own home rentals agency. She likes to be her own boss. When asked why she doesn't start her new life now, she smiles and says: 'Not have money.'

This conversation with Nee raised several questions: Why did Hans break off the relationship for no apparent reason? Surely she must have saved some money if she received US$10,000 during a seven month period? Also it seemed odd that a woman would start this kind of work at the relatively mature age of forty.

Nok, a local seamstress and a friend of Nee's, says Nee had been working in bars 'for many years' (not just twelve months). Nok says that Nee returned to work in the sex trade only three weeks after Hans returned to Germany. Therefore Hans transferred nearly US$4,000 to Nee while she was selling herself to other men.

It does not take a major leap of imagination to consider that Hans may have discovered Nee's deceit before he ended the relationship. Perhaps Hans hired a private detective to check up on his fiancé's lifestyle? Or maybe one of his friends discovered her deception and reported it to Hans.

Later, other discrepancies in Nee's story came to light. Nee bore two children, not one child, with her Thai husband who has since divorced her. Furthermore she is currently legally married to a Singaporean man. This fact remained carefully hidden from her 'boyfriends', including Hans. Inevitably such information would be gleaned during a basic background check.

Nok was extremely cooperative in contributing to the reality of Nee's story. Perhaps the fact that Nee stole Nok's money helped. Another interesting fact revealed by Nok is that throughout Nee's relationship with Hans, she had a Thai boyfriend. She still has the same Thai boyfriend today.

Lying and cheating are integral aspects of a bargirl's function and Nee is highly proficient at these tasks. Bargirls are purveyors of illusions and it is necessary for them to lie, otherwise the obese old man will never feel like David Beckham!

## FACT 2: BARGIRLS ARE ENTREPRENEURS

The following story is based on author Ken Klein's essay which is published in his book *Building a House in Thailand*.

An attractive young bargirl called Sue Lyn had been developing her client list for five years. She had marriage proposals, but turned them down because work was more lucrative than nuptials.

Sue Lyn has five different boyfriends: two from England and one each from Sweden, Germany and Venezuela. Each boyfriend sent her a monthly allowance, ranging from 20,000 to 50,000 baht, so she could stop working at the bar. The largest amount came from the Swede. The Venezuelan was the easiest customer because he rarely visited her. He provided her with a luxury apartment but only used it one week each year. When none of her boyfriends were in town, Sue Lyn returned to work at the bar, where she fished for new monthly 'boyfriends' and 'short-time' customers.

Here is a breakdown of Sue Lyn's monthly allowances:

| ORIGIN OF REMITTANCES | AMOUNT (BAHT) / MONTH |
|---|---|
| Sweden | 50,000 |
| England (#1) | 40,000 |
| Venezuela | 35,000 |
| England (#2) | 30,000 |
| Germany | 20,000 |
| TOTAL | Baht 175,000 per month<br>USUS$5,000 per month |

Sometimes her boyfriends would volunteer, or could be coerced into sending some extra money. Also, she earned additional money from short-time customers at the bar when her boyfriends were out of town, which was about forty-two weeks each year. Sue Lyn probably earned around US$75,000 per annum. That's a tax-free fortune in a land of fifty-cent lunches and two-dollar taxi rides.

In December Sue Lyn received a troublesome surprise. Three of her boyfriends came to visit her during the same week. Both of the Englishmen were to stay in the same hotel and the Venezuelan wanted to stay at her apartment.

Sue Lyn turned off her phone and abandoned Bangkok for the seclusion of her mother's house in the countryside of Khon Kaen. Nobody would be able to find her there apart from her Thai husband. She waited two days, enough time for the boyfriends to be suitably worried before assigning a lady friend of hers to meet them in Bangkok.

'There was an accident. Sue Lyn was on her way to see you when the car went off the road, ' was what her friend told them. 'No, I do not know the name of the hospital. No, Sue Lyn in hospital for a long time. No, she lost phone. Sue Lyn is so sorry, she wanted to see you … really (*jing jing*). Oh, also, she need you to pay hospital bill.'

During the month of December Sue Lyn cleared over 400,000 baht, or US$11,000, without having to do a day's work.

When Ken Klein heard Sue Lyn's story, he told her that she could have done better by saying that she was driving and was therefore responsible for the damage to the car. She had already thought of that strategy. When Ken smiled and asked her why she didn't employ his suggested tactic, she gave him a stern look. 'I'm not like that!' she said, seemingly offended.

## FACT 3: TECHNOLOGY BLESSES ENTERPRISING BARGIRLS

Bargirls are blessed by global capitalism and technology in many ways. The 'switched on' bargirl has access to internet, email, mobile telephony and more.

### Email

Now bargirls 'cut and paste' love messages to email to their 'boyfriends' in different parts of the world, while others outsource such administration to 'scribes'.

### Skype

Bargirls can phone their clients via internet software, Skype, free of charge; technology enables them to enhance the illusion that their clients are neighbours.

## Internet

Some highly commercial Thai ladies promote themselves on dozens of different dating websites to lure foreign men from all over the world. These ladies are usually able to register with online dating sites free of charge.

## Mobile Telephony

Thai ladies love the smallest and most sophisticated mobile phones; and some bargirls own several of them. Many bargirls have a mobile for their Thai boyfriend, another phone for their family and a third for foreign customers. Their foreign boyfriends usually buy the phones for them, so they can send them SMS requests for emergency funds.

## Viagra

The multi-billion-dollar market for peddling Viagra opens up commercial opportunities for bargirls if they are willing to spend time with older men who were previously 'retired'. Usually it's the older bargirls who benefit from this emerging market in the bar trade.

## Cheap Flights

The reduction in cost of international flights is a catalyst for a massive increase in foreign visitors. According to The Tourism Authority of Thailand, the number of tourist arrivals has increased one hundred and forty-twofold to 11.5 million since 1960.

## Support

Now the opportunists of the bar trade are allowed access to free education at Empower Foundation, an international NGO which aims to empower sex workers. The foundation provides language classes and training in various aspects of their profession: from sexual hygiene to customer servicing and etiquette. Empower even gives away free condoms.

There are several technological factors which serve the interests of bargirls, enabling them to save (and increase) their tax-free income.

---

**Case Study: How To Manage Bargirls**

The Number 1 Bar in Chiang Mai was profiled in Philip Wylie's book *How To Establish A Successful Business In Thailand* (Paiboon Publishing) as an example of a successfully run Thai–*farang* joint venture.

Since Philip Wylie's interview, owners Freddy Laureys and his Thai wife, Joi, have established a massive new bar/bistro opposite their original bar. The bar/bistro offers imported draft beers, food, coffee, and wifi access with privacy and comfort. The couple employs two managers who help oversee the operation of both venues.

Number 1 Bar employs some twenty-five girls, mainly between the ages of twenty and thirty. Over ninety percent of the ladies come from Issan, Thailand's impoverished northeast territory. The majority of the ladies have at least one child to support. Most of the recruits, who have previous experience in bar work, aim to remit at least 5,000 baht (US$150) each month to their families.

Joi says that five of their girls left with their *farang* boyfriends during January 2008. However, the staff fills the vacancies quickly by circulating the message on their Issan grapevine. Freddy explains, 'You take one from a certain village, and it's

---

like a snowball effect. "Oh, I found a job in Chiang Mai, the salary is OK ..." It works like that.' A recommendation to work in the bar by a loyal member of staff is a strong guarantee, because the girl making the recommendation does not want to lose face if the new employee fails.

Top earning bargirls working at Number 1 Bar earn in excess of 100,000 baht (nearly US$3,000) per month—probably twenty times what they could earn in the Northeast. Freddy states, 'You have ladies who get money from three or four countries coming in. If you have four boyfriends who send 10,000 a month, that's already 40,000. You cannot imagine how much money they can make.' In Pattaya and Phuket, some exceptionally commercial bargirls earn over 300,000 baht (US$8,500) per month.

Number 1 Bar always gives their staff a three day trial period. They are closely supervised by their manager. After this time, a decision is made on whether to hire them permanently. Initially recruits are designated responsibility for just one table and later their territory is expanded as they gain experience and confidence. Usually after a week, a new girl is able to handle five or more tables.

A point that sets Number 1 Bar apart from other similar bars is that the girls are trained not to hassle the customers to buy them a drink. It is up to the customer to decide whether he wants to talk with the girls and potentially buy them a drink. Freddy states, 'That's a switch we have to make with many of the girls. That's also Joi's job ... to make them understand that there is no hassling inside [the bar].'

Bargirls often attract several foreign suitors. The girls

frequently ask Joi whether she thinks a *farang* man would be a good partner for a more serious relationship. 'Some customers they come to ask me also, "What do you think about this girl? I want to be with her." Sometimes it's very hard for me,' explains Joi.

But not all of the ladies are seeking rich *farang* husbands; some are saving up to build houses or start their own business. 'They have dreams also,' Freddy reminds us. Clearly Mr Laureys is living out his own dream and seems to be helping many girls from humble backgrounds to realize theirs.

For further information about Number 1 Bar and their beautiful ladies, refer to their websites at *http://www.nr1pub.com* and *http://www.number1barthailand.com*.

## SUMMARY

- Bargirls are entrepreneurs and they understand that they earn more money if they tell lies;
- Modern technology is a commercial blessing for entrepreneurial bargirls who can amass a tax-free fortune quickly.

# PAY-AS-YOU-GO LOVE

*Got divorced (wife took everything except the underwear I was wearing)*
*Came to Thailand (as far away from the ex as my credit card could take me)*
*Met a lovely Thai girl (who treated me like a king from the moment I met her)*
*Decided to live common-law with her (don't want another nasty marriage so soon)*
*Broke up with her the next morning (only lost US$30 in the settlement!)*
*Met another lovely Thai girl (that treated me like a king from the moment I met her)*
*Decided to live common-law with her (don't want another nasty marriage so soon)*
*Broke up with her the next morning (only lost US$30 in the settlement!)*
*... repeat nightly until the bad memories from home go away*

POSTED ON THAIVISA.COM

## Pay-As-You-Go (PAYG) Love

An attractive Asian lady, sitting alone in a Bangkok nightclub, was approached by an American man. He introduced himself, 'Good evening, my name is Ken. Do you mind if I join you?' She replied, 'I am sorry but I am not for sale ... but I am available for rent, if you are interested?'

PAYG Love is the consumer-driven approach to relationships, absolutely consistent with modern living. It is perfectly aligned with free market economics. It's also fun and convenient, fulfilling the needs of both the buyer and seller. Actually, it satisfies everyone except the morally self-righteous, the sexually repressed and religious fanatics.

PAYG Love is consistent with spiritual philosophy, which suggests that emotional attachment is the cause of all pain and suffering. PAYG Love dispenses with emotions, and focuses on real sexual needs and economic needs. A Hawaiian expat referred to PAYG Love as 'mutual exploitation'.

Referring to the quotation 'When you're given a lemon, make lemonade', author Jerry Hopkins remarks, 'I think that the guys and the girls who work in the bars—sex workers—make better lemonade than most people elsewhere.' Good girls, who are ideal marriage partners, don't always make the best lemonade!

Not everyone is ready for a serious committed relationship with a single partner. It's ok to enjoy PAYG entertainment as long as nobody gets hurt. This means that both parties should respect and take care of each other for the duration of the contract. Both parties should be adult (not underage) and consent to whatever they do together.

In PAYG relationships there is potential danger for customers to mistake the illusion for reality. Regardless of what the lady says, a bald guy with five chins and a large potbelly is probably not really attractive.

Barry Sandal, author of *Foreign Relations*, a witty guide book about Thai–*farang* PAYG relationships in Thailand, reveals his secrets to survival in love in this chapter.

# WHERE TO FIND PAYG LOVE

### Meeting Places

The most obvious place for meeting sex workers in Thailand is in bars. However there are several alternative places, including:

- Virtual meeting places
- Escort agencies
- Massage parlours
- Karaoke bars
- Nightclubs
- Brothels

For further information about virtual meeting places, refer to the chapter 'Finding Love Online'.

Escort agencies are advertised in the classified section of *Bangkok Post*. These agencies, which tend to be expensive, offer classy ladies who could pass as your girlfriend. Refer to 'The Courtesans' in the chapter 'Love Contracts'.

Masseuses sometimes, but not always, are willing to meet clients outside of their day job. If she likes you, and you get on well together, you can ask her out for a date. If you just want some fun, be sure to tell her that you are happily married.

Karaoke bars, which are popular with Koreans and Japanese, are expensive places to meet ladies. There is no guarantee that the lady who pours your drinks will choose to leave with you afterwards.

Nightclubs are often frequented by freelance 'hunters'. The contract between you and the predator should be negotiated in advance. Although there are no bar fines to pay, there can be added risk of disease or robbery.

## SEX-WORK BY NUMBERS

According to K. Archavanitkul at Mahidol University, Thailand has between 150,000 and 200,000 prostitutes, of which 36,000 are children. The Center for the Protection of Children's Rights (CPCR) estimates the number of Thai and foreign child prostitutes (under eleven years old) to be 800,000 out of a total two million prostitutes in 1996. An estimated 20,000 establishments employed about 700,000 sex workers. About 30,000 underground sex establishments employed about 1.3 million sex workers.

In CPCR's sex survey of Thailand, eighty-one percent of soldiers had visited a prostitute within the past six months. Also the median number of visits during the previous six months ranged from two (for students) to five (for soldiers). A survey of military conscripts from the north of Thailand revealed that seventy-three percent of them lost their virginity with a prostitute and ninety-seven percent regularly visit prostitutes. It is estimated that half a million Thai men use sex workers every day.

The above numbers do not include freelance operators who earn extra pocket money at clubs, shopping malls, restaurants and elsewhere; nor do they encompass predatory women who target *farang* as potential husbands for their career as a housewife.

## SEXUAL ECONOMICS

Bargirls either work for the bar owner on a freelance basis or as salaried employees. Typically the salaries earned by bargirls range from 2,000 baht (US$60) to 6,000 baht (US$200) per month (not to be confused with earnings; their main earnings derive from tips).

Bargirls, either employees or freelancers, can earn around US$1 for each drink bought for them by customers. Typically a bargirl will be given 150 drinks each month. Also the bar usually pays them fifty percent of the US$10 to US$15 bar fine paid by the customer for taking the lady away from the premises during her working hours. Of course the tips are not declared to their employers.

Some men avoid paying the bar fine by exchanging personal contact information with the bargirl and negotiating a deal with her outside the bar, often outside of working hours. The bar will not offer customers any protection if they avoid payment of the bar's fine.

According to Liz, who works with Empower Foundation, bar owners usually dock the bargirl's pay by five baht for each minute they are late for work. Many bars impose a minimum quota of ten bar fines each month.

The tax-free earnings of bargirls can be substantial. Many bargirls and go-go dancers earn between US$1,000 and US$2,000 each month. They are outside the system, so there is no mind-numbing paperwork to worry about.

There are no company perks for sex workers; they do not have social insurance. Workers in the entertainment industry usually have no health and safety protection. To cap it all, they can be locked up in jail for thirty days or fined US$150 for doing their job.

## BAR ROOM DYNAMICS

The most common method of meeting attractive ladies for a PAYG relationship is to walk into a bar and introduce yourself. The acceptable protocol is to smile, be polite and funny. Don't be serious, just have fun.

### The 'Open Arms' Technique

Says Barry Sandal: 'Finding love in Thailand is so easy. In Pattaya, I just drink some beer, walk down a *soi* (road) and hold my arms out, just to see what happens. I never make it to the end of the *soi* without several girls pulling me this way or that. Come on baby, come, come! Finally one of the beauties pulls me the right way. That's a good pull! I'll follow this pull! See where it goes.'

### Namecards

Another of Barry Sandal's favourite techniques for meeting ladies is handing out namecards in shopping malls. Barry's friend printed 300 namecards which promoted himself as a Hollywood film director. After a couple of hours of canvassing in the local shopping malls, he received several phone calls from enthusiastic young ladies.

## GUIDELINES

### Bargirls

According to Barry Sandal, 'Bargirls know how to make money but they've got to be the most fun girls to play with in the entire world. They're lighthearted. But some *farang* men just can't let go of them.'

Barry's golden rules are worth repeating: Come to Thailand and be happy! Smile! If you've agreed to pay some money, pay it. Don't make a problem. Don't break the law. Then go home unmarried. Don't fall in love with them. Don't buy them a house or a car. Easy!

These girls are not stupid but they are uneducated, so after a couple of hours there may not be much to talk about.

## Hunters

Some of these girls are commercial predators. Barry calls these girls hunters. 'I know one called Nok—she's a friend of my girlfriend—and she targets foreign men who are over sixty. She prefers French men. She zones in on guys who have been in town for just a week or two; she never bothers guys who have been in Thailand for a year or so.'

Hunters are not interested in men under sixty because such guys usually want too much sex or ask too many questions. Older men have more money to share and less energy to spare. Hunters are commercially savvy and efficient in their job. Once the hunter attaches to her prey, she'll use the disarming magic words 'I love you! I love you! I love you!' until she has him in her pocket.

## Playing The Game

Barry Sandal dedicated his book to his friend Charlie. According to Barry, 'Charlie, who is seventy-three years old, has at least three different ladies each week. He also has a steady girlfriend. He's always smiling and joking.

'Once I was with Charlie at his apartment when a girl came to see him. Charlie didn't like her appearance so he pulled out his wallet and said "I'm really sorry darling but you are not exactly as I expected. I want you to have some money because I know you have come a long way to see me." That girl was so happy. Afterwards she would bring her friends along to him and say, "I know you don't like me but maybe you will like my friend." They all love Charlie because he always plays their game.'

Get to know the illusion, tame it and play the game. The girls keep saying 'I love you!' and I reply 'You're twenty years old and beautiful and you love me? I know it's not true but it sounds so good, so please don't stop saying that!' But many guys really believe it and get burnt badly.

I have heard of men who have just five seconds of sex with their woman. The next morning the woman says 'That was the best! You are number one!' They are so convincing.

## COMMON MISTAKES

### Refunds

Many *farang* men make the mistake of thinking they can outsmart the girl and get their money back but they can't. Such guys should cut their losses as soon as possible and walk away feeling grateful for the fun they had. They should take responsibility for their mistakes and move on.

Martin invested US$20,000 in a business with a Thai lady. Later he discovered that the woman wasn't the girl of his dreams. She had four other *lukka* (customers) and their ATM cards. So he thought, 'Well, if I keep playing her along, maybe I will get a chance to claw back my money somehow.' But she knows his game and he keeps spending money on her, a bit like investing in a bad business.

Another big mistake is refusing to pay the girl if she doesn't do whatever the man wants. Maybe she doesn't want to do anything. So he tells her to leave without giving her anything. Why? It's only 1,000 baht! Now he's created a problem for himself. Her friends may come after him when he visits that bar again and the bar won't be happy with him either. Retribution can be painfully harsh.

### Judgment

Most *farang* confuse themselves (and all the Thai ladies around them) by introducing their judgmental mindset to a culture where acceptance prevails. Foreign people often think: This is right and that is wrong! Thais have no such fixed perceptions of 'right' or 'wrong'. There is no black or white in Thailand, just a grey scale that never ends without 'right' or 'wrong' at either end—only different shades of grey. Then a newbie *farang* might come along and tell everyone he meets how they should live their lives. It's better to drop the judgmental attitude and have fun instead.

## The 'Accidental' Meeting

An American dentist called David showed me a photograph of his new Thai girlfriend. She was drop-dead gorgeous, probably the most beautiful woman I had ever seen. I asked him if he met her in a bar. 'In a bar?' 'Oh no!' he replied, 'It was by accident. I met her at the mall in Pattaya. She walked up to me and asked me for something.'

Within a few weeks of this 'accidental' meeting, he bought her a house, new car and furniture for the entire family. He also got her pregnant. He was perfectly happy to support her parents, brothers and sisters.

Later he had suspicions about her lifestyle so he instructed a private detective to keep an eye on her. Soon afterwards he received evidence that she was only seventeen years old (underage) and 'working' several other *farang* men.

David looked for a way out. The DNA test revealed that he was indeed the father of her baby. However, he tried to reclaim the house on the grounds that she had misrepresented her age.

The point of this story is: there is no such thing as an accidental meeting in Pattaya. David's accidental meeting was premeditated by a predator. David's advice to *farang* men searching for love is, 'If a

Thai woman comes after you, watch out!'

## EMPOWERING SEX WORKERS

### Empower Foundation

There are several NGOs working with sex workers in Southeast Asia, including Empower Foundation, a support center and rights organization formed in 1984 for sex workers.

Empower Foundation aims to change public perception about the role of sex work in society. This international foundation's message is that sex workers offer an important service to society; the sex workers who choose this type of work are not victims. 'It's just a job which should be recognized as such' is the bottom-line message.

Liz, who works with Empower, asks, 'Why shouldn't the service of fulfilling a person's sexual needs be recognized as work?' One possible answer to this question is that certain religions have yet to recognize that many human beings do have sexual needs.

The business of sex has not been decriminalized in Thailand, unlike in Nevada (USA), Victoria (Australia), Amsterdam (Holland) and Singapore (where prostitution has always been legal within certain parameters). However, Empower does not want the sex trade to be legalized, because legality would mean lower earnings, taxes and bureaucracy.

The foundation does want protection of its members from unscrupulous bosses and authorities; so sex workers continue to earn high 'illegal (tax-free) earnings' while receiving legal protection and state benefits for work they choose to do.

Currently in Thailand, women who work in bars, brothels, massage parlours and similar entertainment centers are not protected by national labour laws. This means that sex workers cannot claim sick leave, minimum wages or health and safety protection.

Here is a comment which was posted on the Thaivisa.com forum: 'Empower does not fall within the traditional western feminist model which views sex workers as 'oppressed victims of the patriarchy' who should be saved from sex slavery. The view espoused by the sex workers themselves is sex-positive third wave feminism; their imperative is 'Stop treating us like children and victims', while fighting for better, safer working conditions and demanding respect for their work.'

For further information about Empower Foundation, visit their website at: *http://www.empowerfoundation.org.*

**Can Do Bar**

Empower has its own bar in Chiang Mai called Can Do Bar, which is managed by the sex workers. The empowered women working in this bar are salaried employees who are not driven solely to serving their customers. On one occasion the staff ignored customers while continuing to apply their make-up. Eager freelance ladies from across the road cheekily lured these customers away; it has since been suggested that a name change is in order ... to Cannot Bar.

Above Can Do Bar is a gallery and museum for sex workers. Relegated to the back corner of the room is a life-size dummy of 'Mr Bad Boy'. Linda explains that Mr Bad Boy never pays for sex and he always refuses to wear a condom; he looks slightly punch-drunk and battered, understandably an object of hatred for frustrated women.

Can Do Bar's ladies' bathroom wall is a forum for feminist graffiti. The words 'FUCK THE FUCKERS!' are emblazoned across the wall for the female captive audience. When asked about the gentleman's toilets, Linda pointed towards the outside yard with a disdainful look on her face. The yard, which stinks of urine, is fit for any dog. Who's taking the piss here?

## Goodwill Foundation

Goodwill is another not-for-profit organization that serves the needs of disadvantaged Thais, predominantly sex workers. The foundation develops the trainees' skill sets, including English language ability and computer literacy.

May, a young lady from northeast Thailand, explains that the purpose of her job is to find 'proper' jobs for these disadvantaged ladies, usually finding office work for them in local businesses. To date, May has a one hundred percent success record in finding legitimate jobs for the women. The only problem is that the women usually don't show up.

The ladies in the Goodwill program are keen to take advantage of free computer and language training but they cannot turn their back on monthly tax-free earnings in the region of US$1,500. Instead they improve their English language skills to communicate better with *farang* customers and enhance their computer skills so they can chat more effectively with *farang* in virtual chatrooms.

The end result: These predominantly Christian NGOs wind up unintentionally helping disadvantaged women become better and richer sex workers.

# SEX WORK

The fact that the word sex work exists implies that it is a service and there is a real need for it.

Some sex workers commented that they are thankful that many wives—especially *farang* wives—are lazy in the bedroom. 'They enable us to get more customers and more money!'

It has been proven that sexual activity lapses after marriage so many customers of sex workers are married men. It could be deduced that women in committed relationships who don't satisfy their men are a primary cause of prostitution.

## TIPS

- Be open about what you want, negotiate a short-time 'deal', and remember that you should never break the contract;
- Read the book *Private Dancer* by Stephen Leather (published by Monsoon Books). A deputy head master at a school in Northern Thailand says *Private Dancer* is compulsory reading for all newly recruited *farang* teachers;
- Do not get emotionally attached to a bargirl unless you really know what you are doing;
- Don't even think about underage sex, or any act which may harm another person, or your fate may be similar to Gary Glitter's;
- For further information about Pay-As-You-Go Love, read the chapter 'Opportunities in the Food & Beverage Industry';
- Always protect yourself by wearing a condom during PAYG love;
- Have fun, always respect and take care of the

person you entered a short-time love contract with.

## SUMMARY

- If you think it's not a wise idea to marry a sex worker from your home country, it's probably not any wiser to wed a prostitute from another country;
- If you really want a serious relationship, your chances of success increase tenfold when you source her, rather than the other way round. If you met her in a bar, she found you;
- Never argue about 1,000 baht even if you think you have been cheated. Just pay and walk away with a smile on your face;
- Don't ask for a refund; instead think of it as a fee for teaching you a lesson;
- Always stick to the deal you made at the beginning, otherwise there may be trouble;
- There are no 'accidental' meetings in Pattaya and other hot tourist destinations;
- If you have US$2,000 to spare why not enjoy a really classy girlfriend for a week—but you may have to queue up for three months!

## Part Two

# RISK MANAGEMENT & PAPERWORK

# THE LOVE AUDIT

*If you detect a single lie, you have identified the 'tip of the iceberg', so change course immediately or you will go down like the Titanic*

PHIL NICKS WITH WARREN OLSON

This chapter is about checking the suitability of your partner-to-be. Relationship commitments have many serious implications, which can affect your health, wealth, social and legal status. A few simple background checks and pertinent questions can help you to avoid the common pitfalls.

Family background checking, investigation into suspected cases of infidelity and the task of shedding light on 'the truth, the whole truth and nothing but the truth' offers myriad profitable opportunities to Love Entrepreneurs. There are some simple techniques described in this chapter which can help to reduce relationship 'risk' and potentially save yourself thousands of dollars and untold suffering.

The famous Bangkok private investigator, Warren Olson, who wrote the book *Confessions of a Bangkok Private Eye* with Stephen Leather, offers insights about how to really understand Thai people.

As with all relationships, the key to harmony is trust. If you cannot trust your partner your intuition is probably not deceiving you. As warren Olson says, you just need to detect one lie. A person who lies once lies a million times. And it's not too difficult to detect just one lie.

## BACKGROUND CHECKS

What follows is a list of straightforward tests to validate your partner-to-be.

Control questions are an effective way of detecting lies. A control question is a question which can easily be checked. For example, the answer to 'How old are you?' can easily be verified against the subject's identity card (*butprachachun*). Checking the ID card is a good place to start because it confirms the person's sexual identity in lands of smiling ladyboys.

Control events are effective ways of calibrating a person's honesty. For example, leave a seemingly mislaid banknote or two somewhere around your home. Then wait and see whether your partner returns the property to its rightful owner.

### Employment
Find out where your partner works and phone her there. To validate her employer it is necessary to make a direct phone call to her while she is at her employer's address. Leaving a phone message and subsequent call back does not count because she could be phoning back from a different location.

### Unaccounted Husbands and Children
It is not always easy to check whether your Thai lady has a husband or children because there is no centralized marriage registry.

Marriages are usually registered at either party's local *amphur* office. However, some marriages, like common-law relationships, are sealed socially by village ceremony and the transfer of gold without formal registration. And some couples choose to register their marriage at a completely different *amphur* office, and there are hundreds of them in Thailand.

Thai people are meant to register their home at the local *amphur* office. They should be listed on the property document (*tabienban*) for their residential address. This property book lists all the registered Thai citizens living at the property. Of course the document should list any children living at the address.

Some Thai people do not reregister with their new local *amphur* office when they move to a new address. This makes it extremely difficult to confirm their residential address.

**Residential Address**

Meet your partner-to-be at her real home address, whether it is registered or not. You have genuine cause for concern if she tries to stop you meeting her at her home unless she lives with her parents.

**HIV Tests**

Most Thais will agree to take a medical examination to check for sexually transmitted diseases, including HIV. But you should take the tests as well even if you are sure you are clean. It shows consideration for her.

## WARNING SIGNS

### Eye Contact

Traditionally, a Thai lady would never stare directly into a stranger's eyes while smiling at them. Such behavior is considered impolite. So if he or she does not return your direct eye contact, it may be a positive sign.

Many bargirls flirt with strangers while walking down the street with their foreign customers next to them. If your partner canvasses for new business right in front of you, imagine what she would do behind your back.

### Alcohol, Cigarettes & Drugs

In the Land of Smiles, many people indulge in pleasures to excess; moderation is rare. So if you are attracted to someone who drinks alcohol or smokes, be wary. In Thai culture, decent ladies do not drink alcohol or smoke cigarettes.

Try to ascertain whether your partner has any close family members who are alcoholics or gamblers; if so, be extremely wary. The addicted family member will probably exert financial pressure on you sometime.

Don't underestimate the importance of chemistry. The pharmaceutical industry is booming, and it's best that the chemistry remains between the couple rather than inside either party.

### Learning Thai

Beware of the uneducated Thai lady who speaks English well as this could indicate she's spent many nights with *farang* men. Similarly, stear clear of a lady who discourages you from learning the Thai language and culture. Conversely, educated Thai ladies with a sound command of the English language—and who also encourage you to learn the Thai language—are probably a good bet.

**Pressure To Decide**

If she (or he) is putting you under pressure to make an important decision about the relationship, back off! The fact that she is pushing for a quick decision indicates that she is either desperate or manipulative. Instead, meet a few other gals. Never allow yourself to be coerced into making such important decisions.

**Strictly Superficial**

Superficial relationships have a short shelf-life; so if money, physical appearance or sex is the main impetus for being together, just enjoy it while it lasts.

**Foreign Targets**

Freelance predators target foreign men who have not stayed in Asia for more than a few weeks. They usually don't want to meet men who have stayed—or strayed—for too long. If they find out you are learning the local language, they will likely vanish into the ethers. They want fresh innocence, gullibility and untapped coffers—ideally straight from the airport.

**Angular Facial Features**

According to an astrologer based in Bangkok, people who have rounded facial features—particularly chin, cheeks and nose—are usually most sincere and loving. People to be wary of (as potential relationship partners) are those with angular features, such as a pointy nose and chin, as they tend to be scheming and manipulative. If she has a square face, she may be a megalomaniac ...

## THE UNTOUCHABLES

According to Yanisa, who writes the 'Love Rules' column for *Guru Magazine*, you should steer clear from the following women at all costs:

- Your friend's ex-girlfriend or sister
- Hairdressers
- Your PA or secretary
- The ex-girlfriend
- The hot professional you meet at a club or party
- A go-go girl
- High maintenance hi-so(high society) women

Perhaps Yanisa is a bit hard on hairdressers although they do tend to have a penchant for gossiping; and they have relationship opportunities in abundance, no matter how entrepreneurial they are.

Clearly it's wise to keep a wide birth from the type of predators who frequent trendy nightclubs and bars. Dating your best friend's sister or ex-girlfriend is the perfect formula for disaster, as is dating your personal assistant or secretary.

It's never wise to date your best friend's sister whether you are in Chiang Mai or Cheltenham, Hua Hin or Houston. And getting serious with a go-go dancer is seriously demented behavior in any part of the world.

Don't date your clients, your students, family members, anyone underage or your colleagues at work. This simple principle should not be a problem because there are over six billion people in the world to choose from.

The list of untouchables should be extended to include:

- Anyone with alcoholics, gamblers or heavily laden debtors in their family
- Ladies or gentlemen who will not to show you where they live
- Your girlfriend's sister and mother

**Why You Should Not Date Your Girlfriend's Sister Or Mother**
The following story is a cautionary tale about poly-amorization within the same family.

Gary, a thirty-five-year-old Briton, visits a family drugstore in Hua Hin which is run by a Thai man called Mr Somchai. 'Hello, I want to buy a condom,' says Gary. 'My Thai girlfriend has invited me for dinner and I think she is expecting something from me.' Mr Somchai sells him a condom, and as Gary leaves, he turns around and tells him, 'Give me another one because my girlfriend's sister is very cute too. She always crosses her legs in a provocative way and I think she is expecting something from me too.' So Mr Somchai sells another condom to Gary. As Gary leaves he returns again, asking for a third condom, 'In fact, please let me have one more because my girlfriend's mum is still pretty cute, and when she sees me, she always makes allusions ... and since she invited me to dinner, I think she is expecting something from me.' During dinner, Gary's girlfriend sits on his left side, the sister faces him and the mum is on his right side. When the father arrives to the table, Gary lowers his head and starts chanting a Buddhist prayer. Gary continues chanting for ten minutes and everyone is surprised at his behavior. Then his girlfriend whispers in his ear, 'I didn't know you are a practicing Buddhist!' Gary replies, 'And I didn't know your dad is a pharmacist!'

## INTERVIEWING TECHNIQUES

Warren Olson wrote a research paper for Victoria University in New Zealand entitled 'Investigative Interviewing of Asians' in conjunction with government agencies. Part of his research focuses on epistemology, the science of reasons for the way people think.

The interview should always begin with unarmed soft questions, particularly about friends and family. The interview will not be effective if you rush in with the direct 'killer questions' which make them feel defensive.

It is beneficial to interview Asians in a restaurant where you can eat together. Warren comments, 'Much time is spent beating around the bush, until finally the birds fly out!'

'Direct or armed questions are not generally the best approach,' explains Warren. 'Thai people tend not to rush things. An indirect approach, working slowly around to your main questions will render better results. Spending time to get information about their home and family is a good way to start, and offering sustenance is also appreciated. Interrogation of Asians will normally take longer than an interview with a Westerner.'

Warren recommends not using negative phraseology when questioning Asians. Negative phraseology discourages interviewees and leads to 'I don't know' answers. For example: 'You don't know his name, do you?' may generate the reply 'Yes', meaning 'Yes, I don't know', whereas a Westerner would normally reply in the negative, meaning 'No, I don't know'.

Be careful when your questions refer to the past or future because many Asians have no 'tense' indicators in their language. This problem can be avoided by referring to specific dates or events. For example, 'What did you do on Labour Day in 2006?'

According to Warren, allowing the Thai interviewee a way of saving face is an effective way of getting a confession. An example is: 'Did you take the money because you wanted to play cards with your friends, or did you feel under obligation to help your family?' Cheating to help family may be considered both responsible and honorable.

Direct sales professionals adopt a similar technique for closing deals; The Wellington Close pushes your target into a corner with words like 'Do you want to buy the red one or do you prefer it in black?' A similarly manipulative psychological approach to extract favour from your romantic suitor is 'What is it you like so much about me? Is it my honesty or my blue eyes?' The truth always flows easier during light-hearted banter.

Never raise your voice or admonish a Thai interviewee in public. They will 'shut down' their communication if they lose face.

Be aware that many Asians will make up an answer rather than admitting that they don't know the answer. Not only do they want to avoid seeming ignorant to the questioner, they want to please the interviewer too.

Asian interpreters, referred to as 'a necessary evil' in some detective agencies, often support interviewees in subtle ways; for example, by flexing the meaning of key words to favour their fellow

Asian. Warren always positioned his interpreters behind his suspect, so they could not communicate with each other by eye contact, hand signals, nods or other non-verbal signals.

### Todd's Biting Questions
There is a book by Todd Hamilton called *One Thousand Questions to Ask Your Lover-To-Be* that helps you assess the suitability of your partner-to-be. With so many anal questions like 'How many milligrams of Sodium Chloride do you have with your Penang curry?' you will be extremely busy, stressed and probably paranoid.

Todd has three succinct—yet biting—questions which cut through all the bull. Here they are:

### Question 1: What is your goal in life (or vision)?
Many Thai ladies have no goals or clear vision about their future. They are grounded in the present moment. A satisfactory answer to the question is 'To return to my parents' village to take care of my parents.' A diminishing number of Thais are prepared to make such a commitment to their family nowadays. If they have the goodwill to look after their parents through their declining years, you have a better chance of being looked after in old age yourself.

### Question 2: What is your financial situation?
Is he or she currently able to support herself and her family, and does she have any savings? If she is unable to support herself then she is probably needy—and that's not a good basis for a relationship because she probably needs your money more than she needs you! If she has some savings, this demonstrates financial savvy and she can invest in a family home as a genuine partner.

**Question # 3: What does your family need from me?**
If the Thai lady's family is either insincere or greedy, take the next exit. Find out whether there are any chronic alcoholics, gamblers or heavily debt-laden family members. Does the family expect a dowry (*sin sot*) and, if so, would they agree to return some or all of it after the wedding? It may be beneficial to meet the lady's parents long before discussing marriage to get the answer to this question.

## SURVEILLANCE TECHNOLOGY

Ladies, especially Thai ladies, love to keep secrets. They are practical people and don't want to make themselves more vulnerable than necessary. But now computer technology enables their suspicious partners to discover their secrets at minimal cost.

It's quite surprising—and scary—knowing what surveillance technology is available. These software applications can be downloaded onto your computer within minutes for the cost of a round of drinks.

The most common items of surveillance technology are listed below. Neither the author nor the publisher necessarily advocates the use of such technology, unless absolutely necessary.

### GPS
GPS enables users to track their partners on computer-generated maps by inserting a small transmitter inside the target property. Vehicle hire companies use GPS technology to prevent theft of their stock of cars. If your partner has a tendency towards straying from home, you may want to plant a GPS-compatible transmitter in his or her vehicle or handbag. If you can't access his or her heart, at least

you can access their territorial coordinates.

The following is a typical advertisement for a GPS system:

*Super Bloodhound GPS Tracker is the essential hi-tech gadget for everyone wanting absolute order and control in their life. It is the prefect tool to record and view on 3D maps the whereabouts of your stray Thai lady or roaming farang man. All software is included. Confirm your doubts for only US$269.00.*

*This powerful technology enables you to upload the geographical coordinates of your partner 24/7. You can implant the candid transmitters in almost any part of your partner's body, mobile phone, vehicle or bag. Easy!*

*Super Bloodhound GPS Tracker will help you develop trust in your relationship. Now you can buy real peace of mind for only US$269.*

GPS technology allows you to keep tabs on your spouse. The system also offers the potential for true love to blossom by enabling your spouse to actually demonstrate their fidelity. How can your love grow unless you are absolutely certain of their commitment to you?

### Password Sniffers

If you sense that something in your relationship 'smells fishy', it may be time to download a password sniffer onto your spouse's computer.

A password sniffer is a software application which enables detection of computer passwords typed into the computer device. Simply install a software program onto the computer used by your spouse or partner. The system will invisibly monitor all keystrokes on that computer and enable you to access the information remotely from your online account.

Password sniffers are useful in Thailand, where smell is taken seriously. Here, a person is judged according to their odour. So if a person has a pleasant smell—*hom*—he or she is considered a good person. Conversely the devil has a noxious—*men*—smell.

How can you possibly be taking your relationship seriously if you don't monitor every computer keystroke your spouse makes? You just need to make sure she isn't corresponding with other boyfriends around the globe. It is also helpful to monitor her bank account online to see how much her customers are sending her each month. Password sniffers enable you to:

- Capture every single keystroke they type, including passwords and usernames;
- Read every email they receive or send;
- View every webpage they visited and know how long they viewed it;
- Monitor instant messages or online chat anytime;
- Take screenshots of their computer screen at any time.

Too many people invest hundreds of thousands of dollars in a legal relationship without properly monitoring its progress. It's like investing in a corporate stock and then not bothering to monitor the results of the company. A password sniffer enables your spouse to demonstrate his or her fidelity, therefore allowing trust and true love to blossom.

**Flexispy**

As ex-Bangkok private eye Warren Olson says, 'The way to a Thai lady's heart is via her mobile phone.' Flexispy is the reason why.

Flexispy is a smart program which allows you to access your partner's SMS messages sent or received on her mobile phone. It is necessary to install a program on the mobile phone which must be compatible with the system. If her mobile phone is not compatible, simply give her a new mobile phone already loaded with Flexispy.

According to the Flexispy website which is aimed at suspicious men, the cheating wife's mobile phone is her Number 1 method of carrying on an affair. The system enables you to obtain a list of all phone contact numbers even after she has deleted them from her mobile.

Cheating wives commonly arrange last-minute liaisons or 'lunch meetings' by sending an SMS or making a phone call. An SMS that says 'need 2 c u so much' is all you need, and Flexispy will grab it for you.

Stray housewives frequently lie about their whereabouts but with Flexispy 'location tracking' you can verify her exact location anytime. Flexispy is totally dependable and always truthful, unlike the adulterous spouse who pretends to be shopping in Central department store with her girlfriends.

Flexispy is a man's best friend. Whereas men tend to favour technological control systems, women tend to prefer to use their superior instincts and communication skills to play the game. According to the Flexispy website, 'A Woman instinctively understands each gesture, smell and every subtle nuance of voice or facial expression and knows what you are thinking. This enables her to throw you off her trail of her infidelity. She also has the ability to spot a hair on the bathroom floor and immediately identify whether it's hers or not.'

For further information about Flexispy, refer to the website at: *http://flexispy.com*.

## THE ART OF LYING

Polygraphs, usually known as lie detectors, are used by detectives and investigators to reveal mistruths.

A polygraph is an instrument which measures and records physiological responses such as blood pressure, pulse, respiration and skin conductivity while the subject is interrogated. The polygraph measures physiological changes caused by the Sympathetic Nervous System during questioning. The FBI refers to polygraph-assisted interviews as a psychophysiological detection of deception (PDD) examination.

Some people are adept at lying through habit. In Asia there are infinite gradations of grey in between the black and white lies. Some lies according to Western culture are not considered lies in Asia and vice versa. For example, cheating in order to support the family is usually considered honourable. Altering a story to save face is considered polite and responsible, so nobody feels hurt. As such, polygraphs are not always as effective in Asia as in other countries.

George W. Maschke and Gino J. Scalabrini, co-authors of *The Lie behind the Lie Detector*, do not believe the polygraphs. Perhaps they need to polygraph the lie detector? The authors claim that the technology is based upon deception rather than science. The following is an extract from their website:

'The person being "tested" is not supposed to know that while the polygraph operator declares that all questions must be answered truthfully, warning that the slightest hint of deception will be detected, he secretly assumes that denials in response to certain questions called control questions will be less than truthful. An example of a commonly used control question is, "Did you ever lie to get out of trouble?" The polygrapher steers the examinee into a denial by warning, for example, that anyone who would do so is the same kind of person who would commit the kind of behavior that is under investigation and then lie about it. But secretly it is assumed that everyone has lied to get out of trouble.'

Occasionally clients instruct introduction agencies to interview their selected candidates under polygraph. One such client was a fifty-five-year-old Filipino American control freak who was looking for a beautiful twenty-year-old Asian lady to marry. His plan was to finance her medical school training in America so she could nurse him properly throughout his old age.

There are several lie detectors available on the market. You can measure the length of your spouse's nose using a de-FIB-ulator. This handheld gadget detects variations in a person's voice tension. The manufacturer claims the de-FIB-ulator is sixty-five per cent accurate; perhaps not as accurate as intuition which comes free of charge.

One Polygraph Examination Agency offers to resolve your relationship if your spouse is straying. The company says they will not solve your issues but they will establish whether there is infidelity. Knowing the truth 'is a major hurdle in your reconciliation process, though we strongly suggest you seek the help of a qualified marriage counselor in addition to using the polygraph.' Another evangelical promise is: 'the truth will set you free.'

According to Warren Olson, it is possible to cheat the polygraph by taking specific drugs. Liars enjoy cheating; and one way of cheating is to bypass the means of detecting their lies. Liars don't need to take drugs to avoid detection by polygraph if they really believe their lies. The polygraph only works when the liar knows he or she is lying!

Perhaps the best people to spot liars are liars themselves, because liars think and behave the same way. Presumably this is why criminals often make the best policemen.

## ADDENDUM TO 'THE ART OF LYING'

According to Warren Olson, we should be somewhat lenient about lying, and accept an untruth or two.

'Often this relates to epistemology or upbringing; the Asian style of saying what they believe you want to hear, rather than the truth', says Olson. 'I have asked thousands of Thai girls, from bargirls to genuine department store workers, "Do you have a husband?" I doubt more than three or four ever admitted to having a husband, and certainly I never heard a Thai girl answer, "Yes, I'm happily married to a wonderful guy." The point here is, they believe you would prefer them to be single, so answer that way to please you.'

'What I advocate therefore, is not to jump all over the first lie you find but to try and discover why it was told. In many cases, it will relate to either saving face, or giving you an answer they believe will make you happy.

'Just like a Bangkok taxi driver would rarely admit to not knowing an address ... he wants your fare, but also he doesn't want to lose face by admitting he doesn't know. Direct answers, as we are used to in Western society, do not often prevail in the East,' says Warren Olson.

## SUMMARY

- Trust your intuition. If you doubt your partner, you probably have reason for being suspicious. If you cannot trust them, leave them;
- Learn how your partner defines 'cheating' or 'lying' because it could be different to your definition. Decide what type of 'lie' is acceptable and what you will not tolerate;
- Warren Olson's failsafe principle is that any person who tells one lie also tells many other lies, so you just need proof of one lie which is off limits.

# CROSS-CULTURE ISSUES

*The general consensus is that culturally 'blended' relationships are more challenging, but potentially more rewarding, than standard 'same-same culture' partnerships.*

PHIL NICKS

Ladies from Thailand are known for being beautiful, well-groomed and feminine. They are attentive to the needs of their man. They offer many of the things that the 'empowered' Western women seem to have lost during the past fifty years. However, cross-culture relationships raise different issues that need to be understood and discussed by both partners.

This chapter focuses on the most common cross-culture issues in relationships. Usually both parties have completely unrealistic expectations of their partner. The Asian lady's hopes and dreams are influenced by the 'fairy princess' in every television soap opera, who gets whatever she wants because she is so special.

Most cross-culture relationships with Asian women fail due to financial problems. According to cross-culture relationship consultant Vanessa Tan, the two major causes of break-ups are economy (or lack of generosity) and alcoholism. The ladies are usually tolerant of infidelity provided they are given sufficient economic security.

## THE BIG ISSUES

### Communication

Fluency in a common language is essential for the relationship to develop into anything meaningful. Without the ability to communicate problems to your partner, you cannot resolve them. So you or your partner must speak the other's language fluently.

For short-term encounters, a common language is not necessary. In fact communicating using body language and sign language can be fun. Some say that laughing is preferable to talking during short-time relationship contracts.

Some of the most harmonious cross-culture relationships are between hill-tribe people and foreigners. Some of the people cannot speak English or Thai. One person commented: 'you don't really need to talk' to make a cross-culture relationship work.

Thai ladies often communicate indirectly; they use hints, signs and symbolism, and friends to convey messages on their behalf. It is considered impolite for a Thai lady to ask for something directly, and she does not want to lose face (in case you rebuke her). Her hints are feminine ways, allowing you to take the lead and give her what she really wants.

### Money

Even if your partner is economically independent, you will probably have to make some financial commitments to her. The man is expected to pay for his girlfriend or spouse on dates. In marriage, most Thai ladies expect a house and car, dowry (*sin sot*) and gold, and a monthly allowance for her and her parents. This can be a major financial commitment.

Younger *farang* men in their thirties or early forties tend to have problems with their Thai partners when they don't have enough money. For this reason, many Thai women look for men in their fifties or sixties. Usually the older men have an adequate pension and spare money to play with.

So you may ask yourself how much money you will need to address this issue. Most people getting married in Thailand put down between US$15,000 and US$150,000 to pay for property, dowry and a vehicle. They also need a monthly income of between US$1,500 and US$3,000 depending on location and their spouse's family circumstances.

According to Vanessa Tan, in Asia, most cross-culture relationships fail due to money-related issues. These relationships are about making deals, so place your financial cards on the table from the word go. Don't commit to a relationship unless you know you have enough money to support your spouse and her family.

Unless you say otherwise, Thais will assume you have enough money to support them. Discussing financial matters with Thai ladies is usually awkward, and considered impolite.

Often the Thai lady prefers to assume that her foreign spouse has enough money and goodwill to support the relationship and her family. She will probably have no grasp of budgeting or financial planning, and she expects her husband to deal with 'all of that'.

### Interpretation

Asians tend to communicate indirectly, so in cross-culture relationships it is necessary to read between the lines. Being in a relationship with a Thai person undoubtedly enhances mind-reading skills. For example, if a Thai lady asks you 'please repair my broken gold ring', she may be asking you to buy her a gold ring, marry her or heal her broken heart. Sometimes it's necessary to 'read between the lies' too. The *Bangkok Post* reported that according to the Abac poll from Assumption University, over eighty-two per cent of Thai respondents would commit a dishonest act rather than miss an opportunity. An Australian gentleman quipped that perhaps the remaining eighteen per cent of respondents were lying; but the truth is that some of the kindest and most generous people in the world are Thais.

### The Princess Factor

One way to understanding Thai ladies is by watching Thai TV dramas. Thai ladies love dramas, on and off TV. Thai ladies are always the centre of attention in these shows. The young Thai man devotes all his energy to try to win over the beautiful princess.

According to Waan, Thai women are conditioned by the media to believe they are much more special than men. They expect men to lavish them with attention and 'take care' of them. The man is always expected to pay for her; it's his responsibility to make her happy.

Many Thai women dream of meeting the romantic Prince Charming who has a good education, wealthy family and business. He is well dressed and connected in Thai society. He will take care of his Thai lady and there will be a fairy princess wedding and they are destined to live happily ever after.

The reality is usually quite different. Maybe a fraction of 1% ever fulfils this fantasy. And many of those who 'make it' have to share their husband with other suitors. Waan believes that their dream of a perfect romantic relationship is influenced by television.

After many romantic liaisons, the Thai lady eventually agrees to marry her man. But the princess wants her husband to continue giving her the special attention she received during the courtship. When he returns from the office at the end of the day he may feel like relaxing with his friends. But his princess wants to be entertained. Then disillusionment sets in...the princess may get moody...so her man may stray ... looking for cheery ladies.

'He thinks he has won her over so now it's her turn to start making some effort too,' explains Waan. 'It's a great shock for the princess, like "What the hell's happened?" and "Why doesn't he continue being romantic?" The princess has unrealistic expectations. She wants too much.'

### Dependency

In Thai culture everyone depends on something or someone, especially in financial matters. Men vie for inheritance from their parents. Self-made men are rare in Thailand. It's considered cool to spend your parents' money or to be given an expensive car by your parents. The women usually search for a rich husband to take care of her family.

Western culture, conversely, encourages independence and self-made millionaires. Foreigners want to be masters of their own destiny, whereas many Thai women want to be mistresses of their foreign masters.

According to Vanessa Tan, a cross-culture relationship consultant, Thai ladies say: 'I want a rich husband. I want to stop working. I want a man to take care of me.' Taking care doesn't mean he has to love her. She just needs the money so she can do what she wants'. Love Entrepreneurs use their femininity and charm to hook an eligible man. They want the shortcut to an easy life—they want to be dependent on a man.

## Respect for Authority and Family

According to Warren Olson, ex-Bangkok private eye, Asians have much more respect for authority and family members than Westerners have. Don't underestimate the importance of maintaining good relations with your partner's parents.

Most Thai ladies place their family before their husband. Many Asians have no pension, so their duty is to take care of their parents when they are old. Although Asians are being influenced by Western culture, most still dutifully support their parents economically.

Many foreign men become disillusioned when they discover that their Asian spouse has somehow manipulated them economically in order to help their parents. Unless parental support is discussed openly at the start of the relationship the Thai spouse may appear to have a conflict of interests. So find out exactly what support they need and decide how it will be provided.

Be aware that the majority of Thai women have a primary allegiance to their parents. Most Thais want to live in close proximity to their parents, if not in the same home. Marriage to a Thai lady also means spending time with her extended family. Your relationship will probably not survive if you cannot get along with her family members.

## Emotional Detachment

WARNING: Loves comes later for the majority of Thais. Most Thais will not open up emotionally until their partner demonstrates their commitment to the relationship. In some instances this could mean a transfer of money (in the form of a dowry or *sin sot*) or property before their heart opens.

According to Liza Day, a cross-culture counsellor, Thais have trouble expressing their feelings. Being emotional is considered wrong. Emotional detachment is practical for survival. Conversely, emotional attachment and generosity can harm business.

There is an old Thai phrase: 'You cannot eat love' (*quam raak gin mai dai*). ' Yet there is an English song which contains the lyric 'Love will keep us alive'—the opposite way round. Westerners say 'When we are hungry, love keeps us alive' but Thais believe that love can never ever fill us up—only money can do that.

Susan has interviewed hundreds of Thai women who are in relationships with foreigners. When asked why they date foreigners they usually reply 'Oh, he's *jai dee*', which means he has a good heart. Never did a Thai lady tell Susan that they loved their foreign man. 'Never once, never ever in my career, and I have interviewed and counselled many thousands of women.'

### Being Present

Thai people can really experience the present moment. This philosophy is consistent with their Buddhist beliefs. As a culture they are very physical people. If they want something, they want it now: 'If it feels good, let's do it NOW!' Thais tend not to make plans. If today works out, maybe tomorrow will take care of itself when the time comes? The majority of the Thai population have no personal pension for retirement; instead, they depend upon their offspring to look after them during old age.

Thais can easily forget their past too. Many, who have had

traumatic childhood experiences, tend to deny their past.

If a Thai lady or guy shows interest in you, be aware that the opportunity is for now only. The shelf-life of their interest is limited. If you fail to grasp their offer NOW, they may be far away in a few hours' time and feel quite differently about you then. Take it or leave it NOW!

To communicate effectively with Thai people, focus on your current feelings and express how you are right now. Talk about how each of your six senses (sight, hearing, smell, intuition, touch and taste) are affected right now. Don't intellectualize or talk too much about the past or future. Focus on having fun (*sanuk*) now!

### Silent Treatment

If your Thai partner is unhappy with your behaviour, he or she may subject you to 'silent treatment'. Rather than openly discuss the issue, they may clam up for up to a month, like a prolonged 'sulk'.

When silence ensues, don't fall into the trap of trying to guess what the issue is about—'Is it because I forgot to feed the dog, honey?'—because you will probably never guess correctly. It's much better to catch up on some good movies or read a good book. Don't compound the issue by reacting with anger.

John Pendleton from California experienced the silent treatment for three weeks. His wife was angry with him for buying her the wrong mobile phone for her birthday. When the ordeal was over, John explained that he could have changed the phone for her if she had discussed the matter with him straight away.

### Appearance is Important

Thais are impressed by physical appearance and polite manners. If you want to really impress a Thai lady, this is what you need to do:

- Dress conservatively and look neat and well-groomed;
- Be polite, respectful and well-mannered always;
- Smile a lot, have fun and be relaxed;
- Never raise your voice or get too serious;
- Always show respect for the King and monks;
- Be generous (*naam jai*), charming and attentive;
- Stay in the present moment and be aware of your six senses.

Be polite and friendly with her friends as well because Thais are influenced by what their friends and family think and say.

## Exclusivity

Many *farang* discover to their horror that their Thai girlfriend expects them to abandon their circle of friends in a 'serious' relationship. Certainly many Thai ladies will not tolerate their boyfriend having platonic friendships with the opposite sex. Such demands of exclusivity can be extremely restrictive and intimidating for foreigners who are used to their independence.

Friendships and social life must be discussed during the negotiations, before the relationship contract has been agreed. The lady needs to understand that that some independence and 'time out' benefits the relationship.

## Some Things will Never Change

Do not try to change your partner, but do try to understand her and find common ground. If you try to change your partner, you may get your way, but later they may be resentful. Accept that there are some experiences which you and your partner may never enjoy together. For example, you may never go rock climbing, fishing or camping with your Thai partner. Don't expect them to change, otherwise you may be disappointed. Some *farang* literally try to train their Thai girlfriend or spouse to do things their 'proper' way. Maybe the Thai way is better?

## SUMMARY

- The most common reason for break-ups in cross-culture relationships is financial issues, so discuss these matters at the beginning;
- Communicate with your Thai partner by being in the present moment and being aware of your senses instead of thinking about the past or the future;
- Your Asian partner probably will not love you until you have demonstrated your commitment to her by way of dowry or otherwise;
- Asians, and particularly Thai women, often communicate indirectly, so learn to interpret her signals;
- Be real about your financial strengths, limitations and obligations, and discuss these matters with your partner;
- If you cannot get along with your Thai partner's family, it's probably time to take an exit;
- If you are subjected to the silent Treatment, don't panic and don't fall into the trap of trying to guess her problem.

# POPULAR LOVE SCAMS

*Women might be able to fake orgasms but men can fake entire relationships.*

SHARON STONE, ACTRESS

Occasionally *farang* men find themselves victims of scams in their love life. There are several 'love scams' in existence, mainly to secure commitment in the relationship or for the purpose of extortion. Love-struck *farang* are an easy mark for con-artists and their associates. This section provides examples of several of these scams. Being aware of scams helps you to avoid them.

## THE SCAMS

### The Conception Scam
The conception scam, which usually follows 'good times' together, typically starts with the words 'I have something to tell you ...' The deceitful girlfriend goes on to explain how you have gotten her pregnant and will need to support the baby.

Several *farang* have busted their fraudulent partners by testing whether the baby was actually theirs. One method of checking involves DNA-testing a baby, known as the 'Buchal Swab.' A DNA sample is collected by scraping the baby's mouth with a cotton swab. The sample is then sealed in a plastic bag and dispatched to a DNA testing laboratory.

The turnaround time for these DNA tests is usually seven to ten days, and up to fifteen days for pre-natal tests. These tests have an accuracy rate of over ninety-nine per cent. Waiting for the DNA test results is probably the most challenging part of the process. If the DNA test results are positive, you have a girlfriend and a baby to take care of; otherwise you have to deal emotionally with losing both of them.

## The Wedding Scam

The Wedding Scam is bound to be a surprise, and you never know when it will happen. It works like this:

Ken returns to his home one afternoon and finds it packed with family, friends ... and monks. He knew his girlfriend had planned a family get-together but he was expecting just eight guests, not eighty.

'What the bloody hell are all these monks doing in the house?' asks Ken.

'Oh, it's a wedding ceremony. Sorry I forgot to mention it!' replies his girlfriend.

'Why didn't you tell me? I'm not dressed properly and I don't have any presents to give away.'

'Don't worry, honey! We are the ones who receive the presents!' she says.

## The Vanishing Housewives

Amy Tan recalls a case some fifteen years ago when several Thai ladies, all married to British men, arrived in London on tourist visas. The following day all the husbands contacted the police, reporting that their wives had gone missing.

The Thai wives disappeared at the same time. The immigration officers asked Amy Tan if she knew where they were. Amy said she could not help them, as England is a big country with a population of over sixty million, and she wished them the best of luck with their investigation.

This case is often repeated, though on a smaller scale. Some Thai women only marry their *farang* husbands to gain entrance to a Western country. Once there, it's 'so long, dear'.

### The Under-Age Set-up

A real estate broker named Garfield was woken up one morning at 3.00 am. Someone was knocking on his door, so he got out of bed and opened his front door. In front of Garfield stood a beautiful young Thai lady wearing a scanty nightdress and flip-flops. She said she was feeling lonely and needed some company.

Garfield claims he felt sorry for her, so he let her stay the night with him. The next day he received a phone call from the girl's 'uncle', explaining that he would report Garfield to the police for raping his sixteen-year-old niece, unless he received a sweetener of 200,000 baht (US$6,000). Garfield eventually managed to negotiate a settlement of 100,000 baht to avoid police custody.

### Bogus Expense Claims

Thai ladies sometimes ask their *farang* boyfriends for money to pay for emergency hospital bills for their family members and other supposedly 'one-off' costs. However, these expenses are not always genuine.

The women who fraudulently extort money from Western customers often pay a scribe to write imaginative letters about a variety of tragic events. These scribes are professional letter-writers who write English well and understand *farang* psychology. Some scribes are actually *farang* English teachers, working to earn some extra money on the side.

Usually the claims involve tear-jerking accounts of sick family members or unfortunate accidents. Of course, a hefty sum of money is needed from the boyfriend to 'save' the family. But the cash doesn't go towards the ailing relative—more likely on a new mobile phone, a pirated Gucci tote bag or another wild night with her secret Thai boyfriend.

### Commissions For Business Introducers

Referral commissions (or kick-backs for introducing business) are common in many parts of Asia, including Thailand. It works like this:

Typically freelancers establish commission arrangements with specific shops that they take their boyfriends to. A girl brings her generous Western boyfriend to a jewellery shop where he buys her a gold necklace. After receiving her gift, she returns to the shop—without her boyfriend—to collect her kickback (which may be around fifteen per cent of the amount paid for the gift).

## SUMMARY

- By far the majority of Thai ladies are honest people.

Nonetheless, there are some creatively duplicitous ladies out there. Before getting serious with a Thai girlfriend—especially one in 'the business'—be aware of the popular love scams; otherwise, you may end up with empty pockets and an aching heart.

# PROTECT YOUR ASSETS!

*That girl of mine, she's always thinkin' gold*
*She put a lien on my body, a mortgage on my soul*

SLEEPY JOHN ESTES, MUSICIAN

Whereas other chapters in this book might save you some heartache, this section stands to save you thousands of dollars.

The following guidance has been written with the assistance of Alan Hall, President of the Chiang Mai Expats' Club, and his team at PFM International. PFM assists expatriates in all aspects of personal financial management. PFM's website is located at: *http://www.pfm-international.net*.

Philip Bryce's basic rule for survival in cross-culture relationships is to keep business and love completely separate ... world's apart. Like oil and water, money and love do not always mix well. This guideline is true the world over but it's especially relevant to cultures where the Western concept of dishonesty meets the Eastern idea of loyalty to family.

According to Thai culture it is impolite to hurt another person's feelings; and better to alter a story in order to avoid sorrow, than to reveal the awful truth. Thais are great purveyors of good news, but they are not known for communicating bad news directly.

Furthermore, a Thai lady's primary duty is to protect and support her parents; and taking money from a supposedly wealthy *farang* partner is considered by many to be a lesser evil than not meeting family obligations.

Most people are wise enough to use condoms to protect themselves from STDs and unwelcome pregnancies; but how many people take basic precautions to safeguard their wealth? The guidelines in this chapter are straightforward and relatively inexpensive to enact, yet they often save people from grave misfortune.

The first basic rule is to split your wealth—or assets—between 'home' and 'away'. Decide how much you are willing to risk in Asia, transfer that amount, and don't expect to repatriate it in future. Like many cross-culture relationships, which are much easier to kick-start than to leave behind, it's easier to remit funds to a developing country than repatriating them.

Beware that in Thailand the legally binding contracts are written in Thai, not in English or any other language. Therefore, ensure you obtain adequate translations of all legal contracts. Most Thai lawyers provide translation services through accredited associates.

The most common and effective ways of safeguarding your wealth in Thailand are the preparation of wills, usufruct agreements, prenuptial agreements and placing a legal charge on property. Each of these legal devices are outlined in this chapter.

Specimen contracts are available in the Appendix; but these should be customized according to your unique circumstances and needs, under the guidance of a professional lawyer.

# WILLS

A will is a legal deed which clarifies the intended distribution of wealth between beneficiaries when the benefactor dies. Whenever an expatriate dies intestate (without a valid will), the state will distribute the assets at its own discretion, usually in favour of the country where the assets are based.

Wills can be simple to prepare, inexpensive (or free of charge) to enact, and potentially rewarding for you and your partner, who will realize that you are concerned about her future security. It can be especially difficult for an unmarried Thai partner or next of kin to claim the right to your assets; and the legal costs incurred absorb their value.

You are advised to prepare a will specifically for your assets based in Asia. You should have a separate will for each country in which you own assets.

If you have any assets in Thailand that you want bequeathed to someone, ensure that both you and your spouse or partner prepare separate wills and register them at the local *amphur* office.

There are three types of will:

- A will prepared by the benefactor him or herself;
- A will which is professionally drafted by a local lawyer;
- A standard public will which may be obtained from a municipal (*amphur*) office.

A standard public will, obtained from and registered at an *amphur* office, carries the least risk of being contested successfully.

Your will should appoint an executor or trustee to administer your affairs after you die. The executor may be a lawyer, accountant, family member or other trusted friend. The executor is responsible for paying the taxes and other debts out of the estate, paying the executor's fee for administration (which may be specified in the will), and distributing the remaining assets according to the terms of the will.

Prepare a list of your valuable assets, including details of bank accounts and investments, and give a copy to your proposed executor. Around the world many banks hold numerous unclaimed dormant bank balances; don't allow your assets to remain unclaimed.

Wills should be updated periodically, as necessary, whenever your financial circumstances or important relationships change significantly. An out-of-date will may be as useful as yesterday's newspaper.

## Drafting the Will

Your will should state how you and your partner intends to distribute your wealth when either of you dies. Typically the wife would agree to bequeath all her assets to her husband when she dies and vice versa.

Thai wives are usually reluctant to sign any document which transfers their registered assets to their husband when they die. One Thai wife was very suspicious when her German husband asked her to sign a will. She worried that he was planning to kill her so he could take back all her possessions.

The will should be written in the Thai language, signed, dated and witnessed. Obtain a translation of the document for your own review.

When a foreigner dies in Thailand, sometimes there is conflict between the family in their home country and their Thai partner's family. The Thai partner usually wants a Buddhist cremation ceremony; whereas the foreigner's family usually wants the body returned to their home country. A major advantage of having a will and testament is the option to state a preference on how and where the body will laid to rest.

---

**Case Study**

The following true story is an excerpt from Philip Wylie's book *How To Establish A Successful Business In Thailand* (Paiboon Publishing).

Klaus, sixt-two, is from Germany. He purchased a US$300,000 luxury home in Pattaya and registered it in his Thai girlfriend's name. Two years later his girlfriend died in a motorcycle accident.

Neither Klaus nor his wife had prepared a will, so Klaus`s girlfriend died intestate. This meant that her estate passed to her parents and sisters. Klaus had to move out of the home he paid for. However, Klaus's lawyer managed to negotiate a settlement of US$15,000 from the estate, though his late girlfriend's family had no legal obligation to pay him anything.

If Klaus's late girlfriend had prepared a will specifying her intention to bequeath the house to Klaus in the event of her death, his request would have been honored. Klaus did not have enough money to buy another home so he had to rent a condominium afterwards. Klaus's late girlfriend wished him to keep possession of the home but there was no way he could

---

prove it to her family or to the Thai government officials.

Klaus could also have registered a loan of US$300,000 to his girlfriend (on the reverse of the chanote title document) at the Land Department. The Land Department would not allow transfer of ownership of the property until the loan has been repaid.

If you have any assets in Thailand that you want to have transferred to someone upon your demise, ensure that you and your partner or spouse prepare separate wills—and get them registered at the local *amphur* office.

## THE HOME

The home is often a significant aspect of the relationship deal. However in Thailand, *farang* are not allowed to own land legally. The majority of Thai–*farang* couples register their property in the lady's name.

Most Thai ladies' families own land; if so, it may not be necessary to buy more land. Usually *farang* just finance the cost of building a home on their partner's family land.

Your other option is to rent a house together; then, if the relationship fails, you can walk away losing just the household contents (including her).

If you invest your money in a property in Thailand, there are three ways to protecting your investment:

- Register a charge over the property;

- Register a usufruct interest;
- Prepare a legal will and ask your partner to do likewise.

Each of the above legal protection devices are explained in this chapter. Charges and usufruct interests should be registered with the office of the Land Department. Legal wills should be registered at an *amphur* (or municipal) office.

## Usufruct (*Sit Thi Kep Kin*)

The Wikipedia definition of usufruct is: 'The legal right to use and derive profit or benefit from property that belongs to another person, as long as the property is not damaged. In many legal systems of property, buyers of property may only purchase the usufruct of the property.'

A usufruct, which originates from civil law, provides the holder rights over immovable property (*a sang ha rim ma sap*). The holder of a usufruct, known as the usufructuary, has the right to use and enjoy the property, as well as the right to receive profits from the property.

A usufruct is a legal method of gaining possession and other rights to a property while not legally owning it. In Thailand, usufructs benefit foreigners who are not allowed to own property. The *farang* usufructuary who purchases a property and registers it in another person's name, has rights over the property (including possession), but not legal ownership.

The usufruct is valid when the Thai Land Department registers the rights of usufructuary on the reverse of the property title deed (*chanote*). Any usufruct contract will not be upheld in court (or legally enforceable) until it has been endorsed on the property registration document.

The usufructuary is responsible for the fees, taxes and any maintenance on the property as if they are the owner of the property.

In Thailand, the majority of usufruct contracts are limited to a thirty-year period, with an option for renewal. However, Section 1418 of The Civil and Commercial Code of Thailand indicates that a usufruct contract can last for the duration of the usufructuary's life.

Usufruct contracts may be time-limited or time-unlimited; and either profitable or non-profitable. These classifications are explained later in this section.

For a specimen usufruct agreement, refer to page 277.

**Rights of Usufructuary**

The usufructuary can perform almost every juristic act on the property except to own the property; he or she can lease, transfer or separate their usufruct right to another person during the period of the usufruct contract.

A usufruct interest expires upon death of the holder, so a usufruct interest cannot be inherited.

In 1998, the Supreme Court of Thailand ruled that the usufructuary is allowed to rent out the property subject to usufruct rights. This means that the lessor does not have to be the owner of the property. When the usufructuary dies, the usufruct contract expires, but the lease continues.

The owner of the property and the usufructuary may terminate the usufruct contract at any time by mutual consent and certification at the office of the Land Department.

The usufruct right passes to the usufructuary's next of kin when the land owner dies. The property owner is allowed to sell or mortgage the land, subject to retention of the usufructuary's rights. If the land owner wants to rent his or her property which is subject to usufruct, the lessee must sign the property lease with the usufructuary, rather than the property owner.

## Time Validity

A usufruct contract may be valid for a limited or an unlimited period of time.

Thai law states that the holder of a usufruct right which has a limited period of validity, cannot exceed thirty years in duration. However, the usufruct agreement may permit subsequent renewals of the contract until the usufructuary dies.

The unlimited time usufruct allows the usufructuary property rights for the rest of their life. This usually means that the usufructuary is allowed possession of the property until they die. The usufruct right automatically expires on the demise of the usufructuary.

## Benefit

A usufruct contract may be a profitable or non-profitable usufruct. A profitable usufruct allows the holder to receive any profits arising from the property. A non-profitable usufruct allows the usufructuary rights to the specified property without allowing any financial benefits, such as rental income.

## The Civil and Commercial Code

An important source of usufruct law is The Civil and Commercial Code. This legislation is reproduced below because it is so important:

Section 1417: An immovable property may be subjected to

a usufruct, by virtue of which the usufunctuary is entitled to the possession, use and enjoyment of the property; he has the right of management of the property.

The usufruct of a forest, mine or quarry entitles the usufrutuary to the exploitation of the forest, mine or quarry.

Section 1418: A usufruct may be created either for a period of time or for the life of the usufructuary. If no time has been fixed, it is presumed that the usufruct is for the life of the usufructuary. If it is created for a period of time, the provisions of Section 1403 paragraph 3 shall apply mutates mutandis. In any case, the usufruct terminates on the death of the usufrutuary.

Section 1419: If property is destroyed without compensation being paid, the owner is not bound to restore it; but, if he does so to any extent, the usufruct revives accordingly. If any compensation is paid, the owner or the usufrutuary must restore the property so far as it is possible to do so, having regard to the amount of the compensation received, and the usufruct revives to that extent; but, if restoration is impossible, the usufruct comes to an end and the compensation must be divided between the owner and the usufructuary in proportion to the damages suffered by them respectively.

The same rules apply mutais mutandis in case of expropriation as well as in case of partial destruction of the property or of partial impossibility to restore the property.

Section 1420: When the usufruct expires, the usufructuary must return the property to the owner. The usufructuary is liable for the destruction or depreciation in value of the property, unless he proves that the damage caused was not his fault. He must replace anything which he has wrongfully consumed. He is not bound to pay compensation for depreciation in value caused by reasonable use.

Section 1421: The usufructuary must, in the exercise of his rights, take as much care of the property as a person of ordinary prudence would take of his own property.

Section 1422: Unless otherwise provided in the act creating the usufruct, the usufructuary may transfer the exercise of his right to a third person. In such case the owner of the property may sue the transferee direct.

Section 1423: The owner may object to any unlawful or unreasonable use of the property. If the owner proves that his rights are in peril, he may demand security from the usufructuary, except in the case of a donor who has reserved to himself the usufruct of the property given. If the usufructuary fails to give security within a reasonable time fixed for the purpose, or if, in spite of the owner's objection, he continues to make use of the property unlawfully or unreasonably, the Court may appoint a Receiver to manage the property in his stead. Upon security being given the Court may release the Receiver so appointed.

Section 1424: The usufructuary is bound to keep the substance of the property unaltered, and is responsible for ordinary maintenance and petty repairs. If major repairs or measures are necessary for the preservation of the property, the usufructuary must inform the owner thereof and permit them to be carried out. In case of default by the owner, the usufructuary may have the work carried out at the owner's expense.

Section 1425: All extraordinary expenses must be borne by the owner, but in order to meet these expenses coming under the foregoing section he may realize part of the property unless the usufructuary is willing to advance the necessary funds without charging interest.

Section 1426: The usufructuary shall, for the duration of the usufruct, bear expenses for the management of the property, pay taxes and duties, and be responsible for interest payable on debts charged upon it.

Section 1427: The owner may demand that the usufructuary insures the property against loss for the benefit of the owner; and if the property is already insured he is bound to renew such insurance when due.

He must pay the premiums of the insurance for the duration of his usufruct.

Section 1428: No action by the owner against the usufructuary or his transferee in connection with the usufruct or vice versa may be entered later than one year after the usufruct comes to an end. In an action by the owner who could not have known the expiry date of the usufruct, the term of one year shall run from the date he knew or ought to have known about it.

## Legal Charge On The Property

A legal charge can be recorded on the deeds (*chanote*) of the property for the value of that property. This means that money would have to be repaid by the owner (Thai partner) to the foreign person before the property is either sold or before the owner could use the property as security on a loan.

The value of the legal charge would normally be the purchase price of the property, though it may be a lower amount. The charge usually represents the amount of money you 'lent' to your partner to buy the property (and register it in her name as legal owner).

The owner of the property is still able to sell the property once the charge has been removed (and the 'loan' has been repaid). If there is no charge over the property, the legal owner can sell the property

159

anytime or use it as security for a loan.

---

**Case Study**

Jack Smith invested US$150,000 in a house with land and registered it in his Thai wife's name; so his wife is the legal owner of the land. Jack instructed his lawyer to place a legal charge over the property. This legal charge prevents his wife from selling the property, or using it as security for a bank loan, without repaying the amount of the charge (or obtaining permission from her husband).

---

## PRENUPTIAL AGREEMENT

A prenuptial agreement (commonly abbreviated to 'prenup') is: 'a contract entered into by two people prior to marriage or civil union. The content of a prenuptial agreement can vary widely, but commonly includes provisions for the division of property, should the couple divorce and any rights to spousal support during or after the dissolution of marriage.

There are two types of prenuptial agreements: marriage contract for people who are married or about to be married, and cohabitation agreement for unmarried couples. A variation for people who are already married is a postnuptial agreement, also called a post-marital agreement.' (Source: Alan Hall)

Prenuptial agreements are recognized by Thailand's legal system, and they will be upheld in court.

The prenuptial agreement must be signed by both the foreigner and the Thai person. It protects both parties in the event of a breakdown in the relationship, from making any claim on assets that where acquired before the start of the relationship.

A prenuptial agreement allows both spouses to protect their separate property. Otherwise, if one of them owns property now and sells it after marriage, the cash may become marital property.

A prenuptial agreement allows both spouses to protect themselves from the other's debts, incurred before and after the marriage. The contract may also allow the couple to determine what level of support one of them will provide to the other if they divorce or if one of them dies.

Prenuptial agreements are particularly worthwhile when a Thai lady leaves her secure job to stay with her *farang* partner in his country. In case the couple subsequently breaks up, the prenuptial agreement should make provision for her return to Thailand with sufficient resources to re-establish herself in a new job.

It is normal for prenuptial agreements to stipulate joint ownership of all wealth accumulated after the date of the marriage (or common-law status); and for each party's wealth to remain theirs until the prenuptial agreement is activated. However, a benefit of prenups is their versatility; anything can be negotiated between the couple.

Many Thai ladies explode when they are asked to sign prenuptial agreements. Their typical response is 'So you don't trust me! OK, then, we finish!' It is worth explaining to her that an important aspect of such legal documents is to clarify financial matters to avoid possible disappointments and misunderstandings in future; as well as ensuring that she will continue to be financially secure.

For a specimen prenuptial agreement, refer to page 280.

## SUMMARY

- Prepare a legal will for each country in which you have significant assets;
- Make sure that both you and your Thai spouse or girlfriend prepare a valid will for Thailand;
- If you pay for the building of your wife or girlfriend's house, you should consider obtaining a usufruct contract to allow you a legal right of possession of the property;
- Although most usufruct interests in Thailand are limited to thirty years (with option for renewal), usufructs can last for the life of the usufructuary (who benefits from the rights);
- If you buy land and register it in your spouse's or girlfriend's name, you can protect your investment by placing a *lien* (or charge) on the property at the Land Department;
- Prenuptial agreements are legally enforceable in Thailand.

# RELATIONSHIP VISAS

*Is that a water pistol in your pocket, or are you just happy to see me?*

PORN MAE WEST (DURING SONGKRAN FESTIVAL)

If you and your Thai fiancé or spouse wishes to live in your home country, there are two main types of visa to consider: fiancé and marriage. Fiancé visas are for unmarried couples who intend to get married within a specified period (usually within ninety days of arrival). Marriage visas are for couples who are already legally married.

Fiancé and marriage visas usually provide the right of the holder to work and access government social services of the host country. These visas are also an important step towards permanent residence and naturalization as a citizen of the country.

Before applying for either a fiancé or marriage visa, consider the option of living together in Thailand. Whether you are able to live in Thailand together depends on your finances, skills and lifestyle preferences.

Most Thai ladies really want to be near their family and friends. Asians often have a much rosier picture of the Western lifestyle than reality. Thai ladies can get depressed living overseas and many of these relationships break up. Boon, a Bangkok taxi driver, says that Thai ladies favour Norway and other Scandinavian countries for residence, but UK is at the bottom of his satisfaction survey; Germany is somewhere in the middle.

This section will examine the procedures for obtaining fiancé and marriage visas for the most popular destinations: United States, Canada, the United Kingdom and Australia.

Visa application procedures to other countries are usually similar; usually the best place to start is the destination country's government website, embassy or consulate. For a list of embassies and consulates for each nation in every country, refer to the website: *http://www. embassyworld.com.*

The visa application process can be daunting and protracted, so be patient and organized. Many couples recommend the use of a visa consultant or immigration lawyer. Visa consultants and some introduction agencies usually have extensive experience of these visa applications. Some introduction agencies also offer visa consulting services but the quality of the services varies enormously.

Be aware that immigration policy and visa application procedures change sporadically. Up-to-date visa information and forms are available on the relevant government websites and their embassies or consulates.

## FIANCÉ VISAS

A fiancé visa allows your partner to stay in your country of residence until you get married. The marriage must take place within a specified period which varies by country; afterwards the visa can usually be upgraded to permanent resident status.

A useful source of online visa information is available at: *http:// www.fianceevisathailand.com.*

## United States

In the United States of America, the fiancé visa is known as a K-1 Fiancé Visa. The visa application pack can be obtained from any US embassy or consulate. The completed application should also be submitted to a US embassy or consulate.

The fiancé visa allows temporary residence in the US, and it is prerequisite for the coveted US green card. The marriage must take place within ninety days of arrival in USA. There are no exceptions or extensions to this rule.

Within the ninety day period, the fiancé can obtain an Employment Authorization Document (EAD) which allows the holder to seek and undertake employment. The fiancé can also apply for a Social Security card after they enter the US.

After the marriage, the spouse can apply for an Adjustment of Status (AOS) in order to become a permanent resident. The K-1 visa also allows any unmarried dependents of your Asian spouse (including children under the age of twenty-one) to enter the country, subject to their inclusion on the visa application form.

The requirements for the American fiancé visa are as follows:

- Both parties are free to marry;
- The couple must have met in person within the past two years (documented evidence includes photographs, airplane tickets and receipts);
- The fiancé cannot have a criminal record and must not have violated US immigration laws;

- Sponsors must meet the minimum annual income requirement (125% of the poverty threshold, which is currently US$15,612 for two persons).

Applicants for the K-1 Fiancé visa require:

- A passport valid for travel to the US with validity for at least six months beyond the applicant's intended period of stay;
- Birth certificate;
- Divorce or death certificate for any previous spouse of both applicants;
- Police certificates for each country of residence since the age of sixteen;
- Medical examination (vaccinations are optional, see below);
- Evidence of financial support;
- Affidavit of Support (Form I-134) may be requested;
- Two Non-Immigrant visa applications (Form DS-156);
- One Non-Immigrant Fiancé Visa Application (Form DS-156K);
- Two photographs (50mm x 50mm square, showing full face, against a plain light background);
- Evidence of fiancé relationship;
- Proof of sponsor's US citizenship;
- Payment of fees (approximately US$850).

A personal interview is required at a local US embassy or consulate.

Further information and downloadable forms are available at the following website: *http://travel.state.gov/visa/immigrants/types/types_2994.htm*

## Canada

Canada does not offer a visa specifically for fiancés; instead Canada grants marriage visas for married couples and couples engaged to be married. The requirements for the visa are detailed later under Marriage Visas.

## United Kingdom

Fiancé visas are issued for the purpose of travelling to Britain in order to get married. These visas are valid for a period of six months only, during which the couple must get legally married.

Unlike marriage visas, fiancé visas do not require the applicant to provide evidence that the relationship has existed for a given period of time.

After the marriage, a two-year UK marriage visa will be granted. When the marriage visa expires, the spouse can apply for Indefinite Leave to Remain (ILR), also known as permanent residency, subject to continuation of a legitimate marriage.

The fiancé visa does not allow the holder to be employed in UK. The marriage visa does, however, permit employment.

It is possible to complete the fiancé visa application (and pay the fee) online. It is necessary to submit a hard copy of the visa application, together with supporting documents, to the consulate or embassy, where an interview will be conducted.

To qualify for a UK fiancé visa, the couple must fulfill the following requirements:

- They must plan to marry within a reasonable period of time (usually within six months of arrival);
- Plan to live together permanently after they are married;
- Have met each other face-to-face;
- Have a home for the applicant and any dependants until they are married (without public financial assistance);
- Ability to support any dependants without working or receiving public financial support;
- The applicant must be at least sixteen years of age and the sponsor must be at least eighteen years old.

Documents required for the UK fiancé visa application:

- Application form (VAF-4);
- Passport valid for travel to the UK;
- Proof of relationship (such as photographs, correspondence, plane tickets);
- Payment of fees (approximately £770).

Additional information about UK fiancé visas can be found at the following websites: *http://www.ukvisas.gov.uk*; and *http://www.britishembassy.gov.uk/thailand*.

### Australia

The Australian fiancé visa is known as a Prospective Marriage Visa (Subclass 300); it allows the holder to enter Australia to marry an Australian citizen within a period of nine months.

Once married, the fiancé visa can be upgraded to a Marriage Visa. The visa permits the holder to work or study in Australia. The fiancé is free to leave and reenter Australia throughout the nine month period.

Similar visas can be granted to 'de facto' partners or interdependent partners. These are known as Interdependency Temporary Visas (Subclass 300), and are generally for people in a same-sex relationship. They do not require the couple to be married.

Requirements for the Prospective Marriage Visa are as follows:

- Applicant must be at least eighteen years of age and eligible to marry;
- Applicant must meet 'character requirements';
- Couple must have met in person;
- Applicant must meet basic health requirements;
- Payment of fees (A$1,390).

Materials needed to apply for this visa:

- Application for migration to Australia by a partner (Form 47SP);
- Sponsorship for a partner to migrate to Australia (Form 40SP);
- Certified copy of passport valid for travel to Australia;
- Four recent passport-sized photographs;
- Certified copy of birth certificate;
- Evidence that couple has met, in person, as adults (in the form of a written statement);
- Character documents, Fact Sheet 79 and Form 47P.

These documents must be submitted by mail to the Australian embassy in Bangkok. The processing time is three to six months. Further information, together with the necessary forms, can be found at the following website: *http://www.immi.gov.au/migrants/partners/ prospective/300/index.htm*.

## MARRIAGE VISAS

Marriage visas are granted to couples who are already married; these visas are valid for a longer period than fiancé visas. Usually marriage visas allow the holder more rights than the fiancé visa, such as permission to work and access to state-run medical care.

### United States

There are two types of US marriage visa (known as the K3 Spouse Visa). The Immediate Relative (IR-1) Visa is for couples who have been legally married for two or more years. The other type of US marriage visa is the Conditional Residency (CR1) visa, which may be granted when the couple has been married for less than two years. The CR1 visa allows the foreign spouse to immigrate to the US for a period of two years.

Both US marriage visas must be obtained from outside of the US, at an embassy or consulate. After arrival in the US, the spouse may apply for permanent residence (and obtain the green card).

All the necessary visa forms and additional information are available from the US embassy or consulate. This visa application pack of documents is known as the 'appointment package'. A mandatory personal interview will take place at the embassy or consulate.

The marriage visa must be applied for in the country where the couple registered their marriage. Visa applicants must satisfy the following criteria:

- The couple must be legally married;
- The sponsoring party must be at least eighteen years of age;
- The couple must complete all necessary forms and pay the fees.

The documents required for the marriage visa are:

- I-130 Petition for an Immigrant Visa (IR1);
- I-129F Petition for a Non-Immigrant Visa (K3) must be filed and approved in the US before the K3 visa is granted overseas;
- Passport valid for travel to the US;
- Birth certificate;
- Marriage certificate;
- Police certificate for each country resided in since age sixteen;
- Evidence of financial support (Form I-184);
- Application for Immigrant Visa and Alien Registration (DS-230);
- Two immigrant visa photographs;
- Proof of genuine husband/wife relationship.

The cost of the visa is approximately US$1,050. This price includes the cost of upgrading the marriage visa to permanent resident status and applying for a work permit after the spouse has entered the US.

Additional information and downloadable forms are available at: *http://travel.state.gov/visa/immigrants/types/types_2993.html*; *http://www.bangkok.embassy.gov* and *http://www.usvisa4thai.com.*

### Canada

Marriage (or spouse) visas are granted to the foreign spouse, common-law or conjugal partner of a Canadian citizen. This means that the couple does not need to be legally married or engaged. Marriage visas for Canada are also granted to partners in a same-sex relationship. In all cases, the couple must provide evidence of a serious relationship commitment.

A Canadian citizen must sponsor the holder of a spouse visa for a period of between three and ten years prior to their naturalization as Canadian citizens. The sponsor is responsible for the spouse's and their accompanying dependents' finances. The partner is allowed to work in Canada during this period without additional visas or permits.

This marriage visa is issued by the Regional Processing Centre at the Canadian High Commission in Singapore. The Canadian Embassy in Bangkok does not process or issue marriage visas. A visa assessment service is offered online through the Canadian Immigration Bureau.

The following conditions apply to marriage visa applicants:

- Couple must be legally married in accordance with both Thai and Canadian law;
- Partners applying for common-law or conjugal spouse visas (and not legally married) must provide evidence of cohabitation and that they have combined affairs

and established a household;

- Sponsor must sign an agreement to provide financial support for the spouse, if necessary;
- Sponsor must be at least eighteen years old.

The following documents are required:

- Completed application form;
- Passport valid for travel to Canada;
- Marriage certificate;
- Documentary evidence of cohabitation, such as proof of joint lease or mortgage, bank accounts, phone and utility bills;
- Pictures, travel receipts or other evidence of an ongoing relationship commitment;
- Written statements from relatives providing additional evidence of the relationship;
- Two passport-sized photos.

Further information about marriage visas for Canada, and downloadable forms, are available at the following websites: *http:// www.cic.gc.ca/english/immigrate/sponsor/spouse.asp* and *http:// www.bangkok.gc.ca*.

**United Kingdom**

A UK spouse (or civil partner) visa allows the holder to enter the country for a probationary period of two years. After this period, a permanent resident visa (also called Indefinite Leave to Remain or ILR) may be issued. If the couple has been married for over four years prior to immigration, and the couple has been living together outside of the UK, the spouse can apply for permanent residency.

The holder of a spouse visa is permitted to work during the two year period of the visa without additional permits; the spouse is also free to leave and reenter the UK during the same period.

An application for the spouse visa can be made at British embassies and consulates; or submitted from within the UK. The application form may be completed online. Ensure you print out the completed online application form and submit it alongside the other documents to a British embassy or consulate. After the personal interview the visa should be issued within one month.

Applicants for a UK spouse visa must fulfill the following requirements:

- Applicant must be married to a British citizen or permanent resident of UK;
- Couple must be legally married;
- Couple must intend to live together in the UK;
- Sponsor must provide proof of ability to support the spouse (and any accompanying dependents) financially;
- Payment of fees (approximately £500).

The following documents are required:

- Application form (VAF-4);
- Passport valid for travel to the UK;
- Marriage certificate;
- Health certificate;
- Two passport-sized photos.

Additional information and downloadable forms for UK spouse visas are available at the following website: *http://www.ukvisas.gov. uk*.

## Australia

There are two types of marriage visas available to foreign partners of Australian citizens. They are known as Spouse Visa: Offshore Temporary and Permanent (Subclasses 309 and 100). The temporary visa is granted to the partner outside of Australia.

After a two-year period, this visa can be upgraded to permanent residency status, allowing the holder to remain in Australia indefinitely, and to access government services and funding.

It is possible to apply directly for a spouse visa with permanent residency status if the couple has been married for over five years (or just two years if the couple has had children together). At the time of application it is necessary for the couple to be cohabiting in a normal spousal relationship.

The following criteria must be fulfilled to be eligible for a spouse visa:

- Couple must be legally married, or able to prove that they are in a de-facto marriage;
- Application for spouse visa with temporary status must be filed outside of Australia;
- Sponsor must assume financial responsibility for the foreign spouse and any accompanying dependents;
- Applicant must meet health and character requirements;
- Payment of fees (A$1,390).

The following documents are required:

- Application for Migration to Australia by a Partner (Form 47SP);
- Sponsorship for a Partner to Migrate to Australia (Form 40SP);
- Marriage certificate;
- Passport valid for travel to Australia;
- Birth certificates of both parties;
- Documents showing sponsor's employment for the past two years (such as tax receipts, pay slips);
- Two recent passport-sized photos of both applicant and sponsor;
- Evidence that the relationship is genuine and continuing (photos, travel receipts and correspondence);
- If applying on de-facto grounds, evidence that an interdependent relationship has lasted for at least 12 months.

Further information and downloadable forms for the Australian Spouse Visa are available at the following websites: *http://www.immi. gov.au/migrants/partners/spouse/309-100/index.htm*; *http://www. vfs-au.net* and *http://www.visabureau.com/australia/spouse-visa-for-australia.aspx*.

## TIPS

- The easiest way to apply for a fiancé or spouse visa is to use a visa agency. Visa specialists, or migration consultants, assist clients with their visa applications, so they are familiar with prevailing laws and visa application procedures.

- If you choose to use a visa agency make sure it is reputable. If you decide to apply for the visa independently, ensure you research the current immigration policies before starting the process. Also be aware that some countries grant visas fairly liberally, while others (especially the UK and US) are quite strict.

- Specialist online forums, including those at *http://www.thaivisa.com*, can yield some useful information. These forums offer free advice by people who have already been through the visa application process.

- A spokesperson for the American Embassy in Bangkok recommends couples applying for a US fiancé visas not to marry in Thailand before applying for the visa.

- A comprehensive online guide to visa and immigration information is available at: *http://www.globalvisas.com*.

## SUMMARY

- To identify the contact information of any embassy or consulate in the world, refer to the website:

*http://www.embassyworld.com;*

- Fiancé visas are for couples who intend to get married within a specified time frame, usually between three and six months;
- Marriage (or spouse) visas are for married couples who are in a relationship together at the time of application;
- Marriage visas are usually valid for longer and allow the holder to work and access social services;
- It is possible to apply for a fiancé or marriage visa independently by directly contacting the country's embassy or consulate; or by consulting an immigration consultant or visa specialist.

# THE USUAL (WO)MANTRAPS

*The only way to be foolish in a love life is not to have one.*

KEN KLEIN, AUTHOR

This chapter summarizes common pitfalls in cross-culture relationships, of which there are many. Many (wo)mantraps can be avoided by negotiating a mutually agreeable relationship deal, protecting your assets and being culturally sensitive.

To reduce risk in Thai–*farang* relationships, it is helpful to read the following chapters of this book:

- Love Contracts
- Cross-Culture Issues
- Protect your Assets!

The illusion most *farang* fall for when they arrive in Thailand is the belief that all Thai ladies are promiscuous. The majority of Thai ladies are extremely conservative and would never consider dating *farang*.

The standard comedy of errors of the milked *farang* starts with marriage to a bargirl and ends with divorce, costing a house, bar business and a pile of money. Before proceeding with marriage, ensure you read the chapters, 'The Real Cost of Love' and "The love Audit'.

Some of the illusions are so powerful, even the smartest people armed with cultural knowledge can repeat the same mistakes. Beware!

## COMMON PITFALLS

A selection of common pitfalls in cross-culture relationships in Thailand follows:

### Sex God Syndrome

Barry Sandal, author of *Foreign Relations*, demonstrates the common pitfall of thinking 'I would never pay for it.' It's called Sex God Syndrome (SGS) and it works like this:

Fred tells Barry he has met a beautiful Thai lady in Koh Lanta. 'Really?' asks Barry.

'Oh, and she really loves me!' adds Fred.

'Really?' repeats Barry, who then asks Fred what he is doing for her.

'Oh, nothing. She doesn't want my money!' Fred replies.

'Really?' asks Barry. 'So your beautiful young Thai lady is taking care of you and you are not paying her anything?'

'And not only that,' quips Fred. 'She was a virgin when I met her!'

'So how old is she?' Barry asks.

'Just twenty-seven years old!'

'Your beautiful lady waited twenty-seven years to lose her

virginity with you, after knowing you for one week. And she doesn't want your money. You must be a Sex God!'

Later Barry asks Fred what they did apart from enjoying awesome sex together. 'I took her and her family to the dentist yesterday. Today she has a problem with her motorcycle so I will help her with the repairs. The bill is only 15,000 baht (US$450). We are also talking about buying a miniature golf course together,' Fred replies.

'OK, so you're getting the sex for free, but you've taken care of the dental treatment for her entire family; paid 15,000 baht to repair her motorcycle and you're talking about buying a miniature golf course as well?' Barry asks.

'Well yes, but you won't see me giving money to anybody!' says Fred.

Fred got into a lot of trouble with Nok. He spent about 30,000 baht (US$900) on her within the first seven days of meeting her. He had to lie to break up with her so she wouldn't lose face. He told her his sister was terribly sick in England and he had to leave immediately. So he asked her to hold onto the miniature golf course until he returns.

Don't fall into the shopping trap. She will say 'You don't pay me money.' 'Well what do you want to do?' 'Oh. Maybe we go shopping!' This is when you should give her some money to go shopping on her own.


### Victim-Saviour Syndrome

This trap is deadly; and it's so subtle that you can be right inside the trap without realizing it, unless you are very careful.

It works like this: She (or he) is extremely attractive. She makes you feel alive again ... and you are sure you can help her rise out of her poverty trap. She constantly reminds you about her desperate situation. For example, her father is sick and she has two daughters to support.

You feel sure that you can change her life. You are her angel, a knight in shining armour, her saviour. This is a golden opportunity to carry out a charitable deed, to pay your dues ... and she will love you forever. Perhaps you will even gain merit for this act of selflessness.

But soon you notice that she is constantly reminding you of her dire economic situation. She is always comparing your favourable situation to hers. But you are already emotionally hooked on her. She makes you feel guilty for the life you were born into. She plays on your emotions and you give her more money.

Having an emotional attachment with someone you feel pity for is not good for your mental or emotional health. If you want to do a charitable deed, sponsor a gazelle at your local zoo, or pay the tuition fees of a bright school child who needs help. But don't get emotionally involved with someone you feel sorry for.

### 'I Would NEVER Do That!' Syndrome

Todd is the model American citizen. He is the person who believes he has all of life's answers ... for everyone. And one thing he is absolutely clear about is that he would NEVER have any kind of relationship with a Thai woman. Todd says Asian women are too submissive for him and he likes 'a bit of a challenge'.

Todd says: 'I am sure there are a few gems out there, but really they are the exception to the rule'. He goes on to explain how western women really 'appreciate' his stance on Thai–*farang* relationships: 'They really respect me more for shunning Asian ladies'.

Todd tries hard to appease Western women, but do they really respect him? Todd's western female friends were interviewed in private, and without exception they said he was a fool, and that they avoided him like the plague. His Western girlfriends also have a tendency to vanish.

### Replacement 'Kits'

Jon is a sixty-two-year-old English retiree, married to Porn, a thirty-two-year-old Issan lady with a heart of gold. Jon demonstrated his love for Porn by buying her a house and 'the full kit' (comprising gold necklace, gold bracelet and gold ring).

After six months of married life, Jon felt the need for more personal space away from Porn's family and friends (who he refers to as 'the vultures'). He slipped away to Pattaya for a couple of weeks of rest and relaxation.

When Jon returned to his marital home he discovered that his wife was not wearing the gold kit any longer. The wedding photographs had vanished too. She told him that she sold all the jewellery so she could take care of her family.

Jon left his Thai wife five times over a period of four years. Each time he left her, she sold her gold jewellery, and every time he returned he purchased a replacement kit. Finally he left her indefinitely on the pretext of visiting Bangkok to buy a gold shop.

Gold, which represents security, holds great significance in relationships in Thailand. A Thai lady wearing gold jewellery is publicly proclaiming her allegiance for the man who gave it her. When she sells or loses her gold jewellery, she is indicating that her heart is broken.

## The Basketful of Eggs

Many *farang* invest all their money into a relationship without protecting themselves. It's never wise to place all your eggs in the same basket.

Pierre, a thirty-year-old Frenchman, had a relationship with a Thai lady called Oi. They rented a shophouse together and established a massage business on the ground floor. Pierre invested all his money in the business.

After two years, the massage business started to make a decent profit and Oi told Pierre she didn't want him around any longer. The business was registered in Oi's name, so Pierre was unable to claim anything. In fact, Pierre had been working unofficially (without a work permit).

As Pierre recounted his tale of anguish, tears rolled down his cheeks. He had given her everything, and then she started dating one of her customers. Once Pierre had invested all of his money in her business, he was unable to offer Oi anything else. Oi was able to run the business independently and Pierre wanted financial support from the business; he became a liability and an expense to the business.

## Dying Intestate

A common mistake of expats is not having separate valid wills for self and partner when they own valuable assets in Asia.

It is better to have a separate will for each country in which you own significant assets. It is important that your Thai spouse or girlfriend prepare her own will separately to clarify her intentions regarding jointly-owned property or registered in her name. In Thailand, wills should be written in Thai and registered at the local *amphur* office.

For a cautionary case study about a foreigner who died without a will for self and girlfriend, refer to the section on wills, in the chapter 'Protect your Assets'.

## Lack of Asset Protection
Enjoy the upside but protect your backside. This (wo)mantrap is so important that this topic really deserves an entire book.

Only transfer such funds to Thailand that you are prepared to lose. Abide by the proverb 'don't put all your eggs in the same basket.' For further information, refer to the chapter 'Protect your Assets'.

## Limiting or False Beliefs
The most widespread 'developed' belief which has no place in Thai culture is: 'If I pay any money to a woman, then I am a lowlife scumbag'. This belief is not appropriate in a country where there are the average family income is in the region of a fifteenth that of the Western world. Money and love are inextricably interwoven into relationships in Thailand.

An alternative limiting belief is 'I am cool and eligible because I can have sex with numerous Asian women without paying them a single baht.' In Thailand, and many countries in Southeast Asia, these conventional Western beliefs just cause limitation and confusion.

## Age Differences
If you are seventy years old and your lady is twenty years, and you think she is in love with you, think again. You are engaging in a commercial contract, and if you are not sufficiently generous, you may be placing your life at risk.

In the chapter 'Extreme Break-ups' there is an account of a

*farang* retiree, whose Thai ex-girlfriend is suspected of murdering him because he refused to give his car to her. The lady was probably expecting a meaningful 'golden handshake' when their relationship ended. Inevitably both partners had their own assumptions and expectations which never coincided.

## Self-Discipline

In the Land of Smiles you are surrounded by irresistible temptations and you have the resources to enjoy them to excess. Thailand is a magnet for hedonists because hedonistic living is affordable, relatively uncontrolled and readily accepted.

Expatriates living in Thailand have more 'quality time' at their disposal, so they need self-discipline to occupy themselves with healthy pursuits.

## Loaning Money

Business is conducted differently in Southeast Asia, compared to the West. If a lady asks for a loan, she may really be asking for a gift. Some words have different meanings in Thailand, and the word 'loan' is one of them.

If you lend money to your Thai girlfriend, you may never get the money back, so it's better to give her money instead. It is also difficult to ask her for repayment of the loan because she could 'lose face' if she is unable to repay the money.

Do not lend any money you cannot afford to lose; and gift money rather than loan it.

## Underestimating the Importance of Family

Asians have much more respect for family and authority than

Westerners. Furthermore, a Thai lady's main duty is to support her family; in many cases, her relationship with *farang* is her 'career' which is a means of supporting her family.

If you cannot establish a harmonious relationship with your Thai partner's family you are advised to take the first available exit.

### 'Doubting Thomas' Syndrome

Trust is the cornerstone of any relationship, be it a cross-culture relationship in Thailand or a culturally aligned relationship in the West. If you do not trust your partner, your relationship is already off track.

Too many foreigners waste far too much time and money on hiring private investigators to follow their partner around. Private detectives are extremely useful for the initial background checks and to confirm your doubts. But what's the point in paying for more evidence about something you already know? It's better to acknowledge your mistake, learn from it and move on.

It is only necessary to collect proof of one event of your partner's cheating or lying. If your partner has lied once, he or she will lie a million times. Once you know the truth about your partner, don't throw more money into the bottomless black hole. If you lose trust in your partner, you have lost him or her.

### Immigration without Support

In Thailand there are many available Thai ladies who lived overseas with their *farang* partner and later separated. For legal reasons, many of these Thai ladies are separated rather than divorced.

Most Thai ladies would prefer to live in Thailand with their family and friends; but many are willing to live overseas with their husband as long as they can support their family and secure their future; most of them want to return to Thailand as soon as they can (or retire there).

Thai women usually find difficulty adjusting to Western lifestyle overseas, so they need a lot of support. Thai women need friends; and they miss the Thai climate, their food and their relaxed lifestyle. If they are sitting alone in an apartment all day while their husband is working, they may become unhappy.

There are many successful relationships between Thai women and *farang* in developed countries, especially where the couple enjoy an enhanced lifestyle and financial security. However, Thai ladies do need a support system to help them live in a potentially alienating environment.

## SUMMARY

- For further insights about relationships with bargirls, read the book *Private Dancer* by Stephen Leather (Monsoon Books) and *Confessions of A Bangkok Private Eye* by Warren Olson (Monsoon Books);
- Limit your exposure to cross-culture relationship risk by learning about your partner's cultural background; read the chapter 'Cross-Culture Issues' and the book *Culture Shock! Thailand* (Marshall Cavendish);
- Before investing too much into a cross-culture relationship, conduct a background check on your partner, and refer to the chapter, 'The Love Audit';
- Don't put all your eggs in the same basket, as Pierre did, and read the chapter 'Protect your Assets!'

# EXTREME BREAKUPS

*Relationships in the West tend to be more difficult to enter, but easier to exit; but in the East relationships are much easier to start, but almost impossible to finish*

PHIL NICKS

As with any relationship, getting involved with a Thai partner can go wrong ... actually it can go extremely wrong indeed. There are several cases of Thai–*farang* relationship meltdowns resulting in murder, extortion, robbery and even severed penises.

The agreements, both spoken and unspoken, that a couple base their union upon (called a Relationship Contract) are crucially important in Asia. Relationships in Asia are based around the concept of a legal contract. Usually extreme breakups are caused by a gross violation of these relationship contracts.

Cross-culture relationships carry higher risk for several reasons: false assumptions, poor communication, unrealistic expectations and ignorance concerning the other person's cultural values. In many cases, Thai bargirls cannot comprehend that their *farang* fiancé's ATM card has a financial limit on its output; and the *farang* fiancé is unclear about his obligations towards his spouse's family and friends.

The following stories, which are true cases, each demonstrate that the relationship contracts (whether they be assumed, discussed or written) have been blatantly breached. The offended partner will likely react violently and dramatically. Whether humorous or revolting, these cases are worthy of analysis and philosophy.

If you wish to limit the risk of an extreme breakup, ensure that you and your partner are clear about the terms of your relationship contract. Don't assume or expect anything from your partner without explicit mutual agreement. Ensure you read the chapter 'Love Contracts'.

It is relatively easy for *farang* to initiate relationships with Asians compared to breaking up these cross-culture relationships; and there are many booming introduction agencies matching prospective partners, but there are no breakup advisory services in Asia.

## VIOLENT LOVE

Sometimes a couple's storybook love takes a nasty turn. There are many examples of violent breakups in Thai–*farang* relationships. In the worst cases, one or both partners die. The reasons for such violence vary; sometimes a petty argument is the catalyst which takes the lover over the edge, and other times there is purely financial motivation behind killings.

### The *Farang* Barbie
One of the most brutal Thai–*farang* breakups occurred in March 2005. Forty-one-year-old Briton Toby Charnaud was clubbed to death with an iron bar by relatives of his ex-wife, a former bargirl named Pannada Laoruang. Afterwards she helped the murderers burn his

body on a charcoal fire before scattering the charred remains around a national park, near the Myanmar border. Charnaud, a former farmer from a wealthy family, had divorced Pannada Laoruang after she ran up gambling debts of £50,000.

Their story starts happily. Charnaud met Pannada Laoruang in a Bangkok bar while on holiday. He fell in love with her and they got married. The couple moved to England and had a child together. After several years, they decided to return to Thailand. Financed by her husband, Pannada Laoruang established two successful bars in the coastal resort town of Hua Hin. However, an addiction to gambling left her with mounting debts, and the couple divorced in 2004.

Toby Charnaud, a multimillionaire from Wiltshire in UK, made a nominal divorce settlement of under twenty thousand British pounds. Charnaud refused to pay off his wife's gambling debts but he did provide child support for his son.

Charnaud returned to Thailand to visit his son in March 2005; he was attacked when he arrived at the home of his ex-wife. Pannada Laoruang had paid her relatives to kill him so that she could inherit his money and property. The vicious murder came to light when Charnaud's family, who had not heard from him, visited Thailand to investigate his whereabouts. Pannada Laoruang was arrested and convicted of murder. She is serving a life sentence.

The Charnaud case is a clear example of financial troubles causing a rift in a relationship and the partner resorting to desperate measures. While this story is indeed extreme, there are countless others in which an otherwise happy Thai–*farang* relationship deteriorates due to money matters. The majority of nasty breakups involve financial disputes.

In Thailand, it is more acceptable for married men to be allowed by their spouses to have non-emotional extramarital encounters as long as they continue to provide financial security to their family. When the financial security is removed from the relationship, there are no Queensbury Rules in the boxing ring; it could be a gloves off fight to the bitter end.

Gambling is a mental disease caused by perceived lack of financial security. Anyone married to a gambling addict—wherever they come from—will be seriously challenged. Pannada's desperate gambling activity was a reaction to her ex-husband's control over his family fortune.

Whilst it's easy to support Charnaud in this case, he did make some serious mistakes, namely:

- He married a bargirl and later tried to 'take the bar from the girl';
- He gave his wife reason to believe that he was not taking financial responsibility for her family (whether true or not);
- He caused Pannada to lose face with her friends and family in the relationship breakup.

Shortly before Toby was murdered, he wrote a short story called 'Rainfall'. This chilling story, which is included in the Appendices, is about a *farang* man who had a similar fate to his own.

### The Cost of Infidelity

In the early hours of July 8, 2006, sixty-four-year-old Briton Denis Gill stabbed his Thai wife in the chest; the wound proved to be fatal. The couple had been arguing heatedly in their Pattaya hotel room.

Gill pulled out an eight-inch knife and violently stabbed her after learning that his twenty-six-year-old wife, Chawee Pimasri, was involved with another man.

After the stabbing, Gill fled the scene after cutting himself in a possible suicide attempt. He returned to his hotel, where police officers found him highly intoxicated and bleeding heavily. A stand-off ensued, with the drunken Gill refusing to give up the knife and threatening to kill himself. Eventually he weakened due to fatigue and loss of blood, and the police took him into custody.

The couple had been together for just six months when the murder took place. Gill travelled back and forth between England and Thailand during this time, but did send his wife a generous allowance of US$1,500 each month.

Gill was on trial for murder in Thailand but the charges were dropped and he was allowed to return to the UK. While in custody, it came to light that Gill was a convicted sex offender in England, and should not have been allowed to leave the UK.

Though it is easy to dismiss this drama as that of a crazy old pervert, it reflects a deeper trend in Thai–*farang* relationships. Gill, or any Westerner in his position, should have realized that this beautiful young women was simply earning a living. It's doubtful she wanted a romantic or sexual relationship with him.

It should not be a great surprise when it turns out that the woman has a boyfriend on the side—typically near her own age and from a similar background. Of course such disloyalty can be painful, but it is understandable.

**Love Me ... or Die**
In October of 2006, Pattaya police found two corpses at a residence

in the south of the city. One of them was a sixty-five-year-old German man named Hans Dieter Witten Breder and the other was a much younger Thai woman of unknown identity. The German's body bore deep cuts to the wrists while the Thai died of a slit throat. Officers estimated that the pair had been dead for about a week.

Based on a note found on the headboard of the bed, it became clear that the German had murdered his girlfriend and then committed suicide. The reason for doing so was that the woman told him that she intended to leave him for someone else. The note also expressed feelings of deep regret that he had killed the woman he loved.

This is another example of an older *farang* man taking drastic action after his younger Thai lover left him for another man. There are several unanswered questions surrounding this story, such as who was the woman and what were the circumstances of the couple's breakup. The end result, however, is a classic case of a broken-hearted murder-cum-suicide.

### 'Cut It Out' or I'll 'Cut It Off'

An interesting fact about Thailand—and one which is rarely mentioned in other guidebooks—is that Bangkok is a world centre for penis reattachment surgery. There is a reason for this: cutting off a man's penis is a fairly common form of retribution by angry wives, girlfriends, second wives (*mia noi*) or lovers. Some say Thailand is also a world centre for poly-amorization (*jaochoo*).

Although no cases involving Westerners have been publicized yet, you should nonetheless be aware of this phenomenon. There are plenty of stories about vengeful partners taking the severed penis and boiling it, feeding it to the ducks and even attaching it to a miniature hot-air balloon and watching it fly away into the pale blue sky.

If the unlucky man manages to bring his disconnected member to the hospital within an hour of severance, it can usually be surgically reattached. However, only in fifty per cent of these cases does the man regain normal sexual function of his penis. A team of doctors in one Bangkok hospital reportedly reattached thirty-three severed penises each year—about one every ten days.

There are a number of reasons for the prominence of 'penecide' in Thai society. Certainly the Thai women's reputation for being jealous and vindictive, and having a kitchen full of sharp knives, is relevant. In addition, the penis is seen as a symbol of potency and prosperity. But perhaps even more to blame is the tendency of men (more often Thais) to conduct extramarital affairs and keep 'minor wives'.

The penecide phenomenon is reality but it does not mean that all Thai women are knife-wielding maniacs. Severing a philandering partner's penis is an extreme measure that is quite rare. It is included here in order to illustrate the fact that there can be (severe) consequences for cheating on a Thai lover, just as there are in the West. The rage and jealousy caused by infidelity—a basic element of the relationship contract—often cause a partner to take drastic action.

If your girlfriend jokes about cutting off your penis (in retaliation for cheating) you may forgive her the first time, but tell her you will not tolerate her joking about it again. If she continues to make the same joke, show her the door because she is indicating the way she thinks.

## 'ACCIDENTS' ... AND MURDERS

Many stories are reported about mysterious deaths involving Western men married to Thai women. These stories involve somewhat dubious causes of death, ranging from bizarre traffic accidents—or falling off balconies—to death by eating her extra-spicy papaya salad.

A common theme of these deaths is the wife standing to inherit significant wealth from her late husband, or benefiting financially from his death. In some ominous cases, the wife was found to have murdered her husband, but there are many cases where evidence proves to be inconclusive.

## A Car to Die For

Paul During, a seventy-one-year-old Danish resident of Chiang Mai, was found murdered in his home on May 25, 2007. Earlier that day, neighbours heard him arguing with a woman, possibly a former girlfriend who had returned to ask for a car he had registered in her name: Anong Chaiyawut, fifty-two, a resident of Chiang Mai.

The Dane was found dead near the door of his terrace, naked, with a bloody nose and a swelling at the back of his neck. Blood was discovered around the house, and police recovered a walking stick with traces of blood and hair. There was also a hole in the door to the bedroom, and the keyhole was damaged. Another fact to note is that the car in the garage, a Nissan pickup truck, registered to Ms Chaiyawut, was found with its glove box open.

According to neighbours, Paul During had lived there for three years with Chaiyawut, and in that time had bought her the car. The couple broke up sometime before During kept the car. On the day of the murder, the ex-girlfriend had apparently returned to ask for the keys to the truck. An argument ensued, followed by a sudden silence. The neighbours found his naked and bloody body lying on the floor.

Police suspect that Paul During was murdered by the woman

with whom he was heard fighting. They surmise that, after being struck with the walking stick, he fell and hit his head on the floor, causing the elderly man to die. It seems that the woman then tried to find the car keys, but could not and fled the scene.

This seemingly senseless murder appears to have been caused by an argument about the ownership of the truck after the couple broke up. As Bill Sweeney says 'After a relationship breakup, a Thai lady commonly demands something for her services rendered over the period of the relationship ... she needs something to replace the lost relationship and security.' When Paul During registered the truck in her name, she probably believed he was gifting the vehicle to her. Perhaps he did not intend to transfer ownership to her but he should have clarified his intentions.

### Mysterious 'Suicides'

Thirty-five-year-old Briton Barry Wilson met his end after plummeting from his balcony of his Pattaya condo. His wife, twenty-four-year-old Rung Soongram, alleged that her late husband had expressed wishes to die. However, she stated that she saw no symptoms of depression, or any other physical or mental illness, so did not take the comments seriously. It is unknown whether Wilson had any debts or enemies that could have precipitated such a fall.

This is a typical mysterious death with no substantial evidence of murder. Such deaths are commonly labeled as suicides or accidents. This case will probably remain an unsolved mystery.

## GUIDANCE

Money is usually an important factor in Thai–*farang* relationships.

Many *farang* men (and Thai men, for that matter) support their women financially. Economic dependence by the Thai women can lead to major problems if the relationship breaks up. Suddenly she is unable to support herself, or her family and children, and she experiences loss of face with everyone she knows. The breakup can be extremely traumatic for the Thai lady, who may view the relationship as a means to survival.

While every man wants to provide his lady with material comforts, it is important to exercise caution when setting up a life with a partner. Buying property or a business in a Thai lady's name can lead to problems if the relationship breaks up later. Refer to the chapter 'Protect Your Ass(ets)' for more information about how to manage your wealth in cross-culture relationships.

There is no easy way to avoid a relationship breakup or broken heart. As we have seen in the aforementioned cases, heartache can lead to some desperate acts. An important aspect of cross-culture relationships in Asia is 'busting expectations and assumptions' both ways. If expectations are not met, disillusionment occurs and a negative outcome is certain.

The best policy is to discuss matters such as financial commitments and infidelity at the start of the relationship; such discussions form the basis of the relationship contract.

The concept of 'losing face' is an important factor in relationships in Thailand, so avoid direct breakups; instead take responsibility yourself for any relationship issues, or create an external reason for being apart from each other.

Don't make your partner feel insulted or ashamed, otherwise they will feel resentment towards you ... and that puts you in a dangerous position. Remember, if matters get really hot, you can always hop to another country; she may not be in as fortunate a position.

## HOW TO BREAK UP

### Avoid Blame

If the relationship is not working out, try to avoid blaming each other. It's better to voluntarily shoulder as much responsibility for the relationship issues as possible. If you blame her, she will lose face and resent it.

Barry Sandal, author of *Foreign Relations*, comments that it's the Thai lady who has the prerogative of ending relationships, not the man. If you want out of the relationship, you have to help her make this decision for herself. It may even be necessary to provide her with incentives for dumping you.

### Find an Easy Exit

You realize the relationship is not working out, so make it easy for both of you. Take the easy way out. Dream up a reason for leaving the country immediately. Your mother or sister is dying in hospital. Thais have the utmost respect for family, so they can relate to any gestures concerning family support.

### Carve up the Pie Amicably

Your wealth tied up in Asia is probably not a fortune, so don't be too attached to it. Share it; carve up the pie, give your spouse a fair share, and leave. Be grateful for the experience you have enjoyed together and try to leave on amicable terms. It's better to exit the relationship as a generous person—with dignity—rather than as a stingy (*kee neow*) *farang*.

## SUMMARY

- This chapter focuses on occurrences of extreme breakups, which are rare, despite being widely circulated throughout the media because they are so dramatic. Being murdered or having your penis chopped off by your Thai wife is indeed an extreme scenario. But remember that most Asian—and particularly Thai women—are amongst the most gentle, loving and peaceful ladies on Earth.

- Cases of murderous *farang* men usually involve emotional instability, jealously or obsessive love. *Farang* tend to open up emotionally much quicker than Asians. Most Thais invest emotionally in their partner after receiving material investment as a demonstration of commitment to the partnership.

- There are an estimated 50,000 British citizens residing in Thailand, a country with an estimated murder rate five times higher than the UK. According to *Crime Reporters* blogsite, an average 226 Britons die in Thailand each year. A large portion of these murders occur in Pattaya.

- Only a small number of these deaths involve cold-blooded Thai spouses seeking inheritance. Many Thai spouses are in harmonious relationships with *farang*. Nevertheless there are many 'fatal accidents' and 'suicides' involving *farang* men which cause pause for thought. It does no harm to do some research as a precaution.

- Limit your risk of extreme breakup by learning as much as possible about your spouse's culture and establishing a mutually agreeable relationship contract. Negotiate, communicate, evaluate and update your agreements regularly. Avoid unrealistic expectations and assumptions. Be careful about any topic of discussion which either of you try to avoid.
- Read the chapter 'Protect your Assets!' Consider whether you are worth more to your spouse's family dead or alive. Take responsibility for your wife's perception of how generous you are. Your spouse's commitment to you increases with his or her perception of your generosity (regardless of the reality). Your spouse needs to believe you are generous.
- Overall, you should take these gruesome tales and let them serve as a reminder to be very careful when selecting a partner, and to exercise caution with him or her. Doing so may just save your life—or your dick.

# Part Three
# EMERGING MARKETS

# GENDER ILLUSIONISTS

*'This Guesthouse is warning our Customers for your Safety and Peace of Mind:*

*1. No Drugs*

*2. No Sex Trade (particularly Prostitutes)*

*3. No Ladyboys ...'*

HOUSE RULES DISPLAYED AT A CHIANG MAI

GUEST HOUSE RECEPTION

Newcomers to Thailand sometimes get confused about *katoey* (ladyboys) and occasionally they mistake them for the genuine article. But, like Pepsi, some folk think ladyboys are even better than the real thing.

Jerry Hopkins, Thailand's eminent journalist and author of over thirty-five books agreed to share his personal knowledge and experience on the subject of gender illusionism. Jerry had a relationship with a *katoey* in Hawaii before moving to Thailand and has been a close observer of the Thai *katoey* scene for over 14 years.

'One of the things I like about Thailand—and Hawaii was the same way—is it's very gay-tolerant,' explains Jerry. 'It's not a big deal to be a *katoey*. Every family's got one. And you walk into a photocopy shop, or any kind of shop, in Bangkok and you might see a guy behind the counter and he's wearing a dress and lipstick and he's got hair down to his shoulders. Nobody is bothered, and they shouldn't be. No doubt there are as many *katoey* in other countries percentage-wise, but in Thailand they have come out and you see them. The *katoey* cabaret shows are an important part of Thailand's tourism industry. It's considered family entertainment, and it's damn good entertainment. I think they're great.'

Many Buddhists believe that *katoey* are the result of negative karma—currently paying for misdeeds in previous lives. According to Richard Totman, author of *The Third Sex*, being born a *katoey* is no more their fault than being born physically deformed, deaf or dead. In his book, Richard wrote about Nithi School, near Chiang Mai, where five per cent of the 1,100 boys decided they wanted to be girls.

## THE FUNDAMENTALS

There are different kinds of transsexuals (or *katoey*).

*Katoey* is a catch-all phrase referring to transvestites, transsexuals, over-the-top gays and cross-dressers. Cross-dressers are men who dress up in women's clothing because it makes them feel sexy.

Transvestites are men who dress up as women more convincingly, and that's who you will see at most of the cabarets in Thailand. Transvestites are not necessarily transsexuals, but straight men who look like women for the duration of the show.

Transsexuals are men who are making the transition to becoming women and by using either chemicals or surgery to accomplish it. The pre-operative ('pre-op') transsexual may have had breast augmentation and probably is taking hormone supplements (estrogen shots), which tend to inhibit hair growth, add a padding of baby fat and take away the sharp edges associated with masculinity. Post-op transsexuals go the full distance with a sex-change operation. This is called Sex Reassignment Surgery (SRS).

Most *katoey* in Thailand are pre-op. They do not take the final step because the operation is irreversible and there is a great risk of losing the ability to have orgasm.

According to Jerry Hopkins, 'A lot of men want a woman with breasts and a penis.'

## *KATOEY* AND THE LAW

*Katoey* are legally classified as men; they have no rights as women and they are not allowed to marry a man in Thailand. Their national identity card identifies them as men with the title 'Mr' even if the photograph on the card looks like a woman. However a growing number of employers and universities in Thailand allow *katoey* to wear women's clothing.

*Katoey* are widely discriminated against by banks, employers and government officers because their sexual identity is unrecognized by law, and they are stigmatized as being unreliable by society. Many hotels bar entry to *katoey*. Many employers do not open their doors to ladyboys because of their negative reputation.

Until recently, the Thai military branded transsexuals as permanently mentally ill and unfit for military service. When transsexuals are hospitalized, they are often allocated beds in men's wards; and when they are sent to men's prisons, *katoey* are most vulnerable to molestation and rape.

Transsexuals are labeled by psychiatrists as having gender

identity disorder (GID). Less than twenty per cent of transgender men are post-operative transsexuals. According to the book *Why Men Don't Listen and Women Can't Read Maps*, twenty per cent of transsexuals attempt suicide.

In 2002, the European Court of Human Rights ruled that post-op transsexuals are entitled to change all their legal documents to reflect their gender change. Although lawmakers in Asia are discussing amendments to the legal rights of *katoey*, it may take time before they are actually implemented.

## HOW TO IDENTIFY *KATOEY*

Although most *katoey* appear feminine, they have certain features which remain masculine; for example their broad shoulders, large hands and feet. Usually women are more supple, and can therefore contort their fingers, arms and legs more than men.

Most *katoey* admit to their real sexual identity when asked. ID cards label *katoey* as men. Masculine characteristics of *katoey* include above-average height, a deep voice and adam's apple (though this may be surgically reduced in size by 'shaving'). Transsexuals also tend to exaggerate the wiggle of their hips as they walk, being such cheeky 'drama queens' as they are.

Most transsexuals are pre-op, so they have a penis. Although Crocodile Dundee got away with grabbing a transsexual by the private parts in his movie, such extreme approaches are not recommended.

# JERRY HOPKINS' STORY

### The *Mahu* Scene

Jerry had lived in Hawaii for about fifteen years before his divorce in his mid-fifties. He was getting 'a little bored'. Within two or three years Jerry would have moved to Thailand to help solve his boredom issue but in the interim he was playing the field. He was dating several people.

Jerry has always been attracted to the 'seamier side of life' and the more offbeat side of life. Jerry explains: 'By that, I am not talking about sex. I'm not talking about drugs and rock and roll. I'm talking about everything from when I was a kid, reading only science fiction. I tended to, you know, travel off the beaten track.'

So when Jerry heard that there was, what is called in Hawaii, a *mahu* bar in a suburban beach town called Kailua, he thought 'well, that's ridiculous! You can't have that kind of bar in a conservative community like that!' So he went to see for himself. Then it occurred to him that there was a marine base and housing nearby. This confirmed his suspicions about American marines.

Jerry went to the bar and introduced himself to the Vietnamese owner of the bar and told her that he was a writer and interested in her bar and meeting some of the people who worked there. The owner was not *mahu* (or *katoey*). She was a straight business woman who had been in the bar business for a long time.

There was a young woman at the bar—in her twenties at the time—who was working the karaoke machine. The bar was full of US marines getting drunk, and singing rock and roll songs on the karaoke system. She looked like a cute Filipina with fabulous breasts and a perky sense of humour. The bar owner called her over and introduced Jerry to her.

'This is Vanessa,' she said. 'Jerry is a writer who is looking for interesting stories. Why don't you tell him your story? Make sure he buys you a twenty-dollar drink!'

Jerry bought her a US$20 drink but Vanessa said, 'My story is too complicated.'

'Well give me the simple version!' came Jerry's reply.

'I was born a boy. And now,' she continued, holding out her chest, 'I am a man!'

They soon became friends and Jerry eventually got her whole life story. At that time she was dating a guy who had gone into the pizza parlor next door, and while waiting for his pizza to cook, had visited the bar to have a beer, not knowing anything about the bar. He started talking with Vanessa and they started dating. He still had no clue about her sexual identity.

Vanessa—whose name was Van when she was a boy—was a pre-op *katoey*. She had had breast enhancement surgery and she took hormone shots. She still had a penis. Jerry referred to her as 'One-stop shopping!'

Vanessa dated Pizza Guy for a while and he still didn't know about her sexual identity. He kept on asking her to go to bed with him and she always refused. When finally she told him, the guy bolted and broke her heart.

Vanessa was really in love with Pizza Guy. She couldn't understand why sex should be considered so important. She explained to Jerry, 'I am a good cook and I just wanted to take care of him and be a good wife.'

Jerry and Vanessa continued to go out together. One night, they went out to a gay nightclub called The Tropical Gardens. There was a traditional Hawaiian trio playing music there. The music was excellent and many of the performers from Waikiki would visit the club after finishing their own shows. There are a lot of gay performers and dancers in the hula community. They would get up on stage and perform. There was a sensational party atmosphere.

Jerry and Vanessa were friends for about nine months before he fell in love with her. Then Vanessa moved into Jerry's cottage 'on and off' over a period of two years.

### Dating a *Mahu*

Even though Jerry began to want more from the relationship, he and Vanessa had a completely platonic friendship until some time after Pizza Guy was out of the picture.

From the beginning it was never a secret that Jerry was dating a *mahu*. All Jerry's friends knew about it. Jerry was working for a weekly business newspaper and his ex-wife was working in public relations in the hotel industry. They both shared many of the same friends, many of whom were journalists. His ex-wife tried to undermine Jerry by telling the journalists that he was living with a *mahu*. Jerry's friends would say 'Yes, we've met her and she's really nice!'

Jerry never had any secrets. As he explains today: 'As a writer, I'm given a lot of leeway in terms of lifestyle and behavior by society at large. So it's easier for me to take that position than most people.'

Jerry has never disapproved of sex for sale. Vanessa and Jerry had mutual respect for each other, and her job didn't get in the way of their relationship. She wanted to continue hooking, and Jerry told her she should be whatever she wished to be.

Jerry became a fixture of the *mahu* scene. They referred to Jerry as 'Vanessa's husband', even though they weren't married. Almost all their social life together was in *mahu* society. Vanessa always participated in the beauty queen contests—of which there were many—and she always did very well. Vanessa's photograph even appeared on the front cover of *Crossdresser's Quarterly* magazine.

### The Halloween Party

Jerry knew a married couple who lived in Honolulu. He was a very successful dermatologist and she was a fine artist. She had a gallery in Chinatown, which was known for its seedy bars, but also for its art galleries. Her husband moved his dermatology office into the basement of this building. They had an office-warming party on Halloween. Everyone was asked to dress up in costumes and Jerry wanted Vanessa to accompany him. The party was attended by doctors, lawyers, politicians and businessmen … the crème-de-la-crème of straight society, with whom Vanessa had no experience whatsoever. Jerry wanted her to go with him, but she was terrified.

Vanessa asked Jerry what kind of costume she should wear. Jerry suggested that she dress up as a boy: 'Your brother is about the same size as you … he's in jail, so why don't you wear one of his three-piece suits?' So she wore this really nice pinstripe three-piece suit with a sexy lacy black bra underneath. Her waistcoat was unbuttoned to below her cleavage. She wore far too much makeup, which was a sign of her nervousness. Anyway, Jerry thought 'what the hell!' and took her to the party.

All of Jerry's male friends 'tripped over their tongues' trying to talk with her. They went gaga about this absolutely magnificent creature on Jerry's arm. She had such a perky personality, so she was a great success.

## Vanessa's Transformation

Vanessa was not happy as an ordinary boy at the age of fourteen when going through the adolescent 'hormone storm'. She started wearing lipstick and dresses, and letting her hair grow long while she was still going to high school.

Vanessa's father was a lifeguard on Waikiki beach and a noted canoe paddler. He coached the canoe paddling team at Vanessa's high school. He asked her to help him teach the guys to paddle. She was teased a lot, but she 'gave as good as she received' because she had some authority.

Vanessa's father was not a nice guy. The family was dysfunctional. Both parents were alcoholic. Vanessa's father beat his wife and kids (three boys and two girls). Two of the boys became *mahus* and the third became a criminal, ending up in jail. One of the girls became a lesbian and the other killed herself.

By the age of sixteen, Vanessa had had enough of home. By this time she was familiar with the streetwalking scene in Honolulu's Chinatown. She had friends in Chinatown and moved in with one of the *mahu* streetwalkers. She started hormone therapy and continued to grow her hair. Gradually she taught herself how to look and act like a woman.

One of Vanessa's *mahu* sisters decided to get her breasts surgically augmented, and Vanessa decided to enhance hers too. The two of them worked at a nightclub in Chinatown called The Glades, which was like a Thai cabaret club. They were called 'female impersonation clubs'.

For a while, Vanessa and her sister were Honolulu's bookend hula dancers for one of the star performances. However her primary source of income was as a street hooker. She would often stand on the street corners of Chinatown waiting for customers.

Vanessa also worked in karaoke bars and would take marines into the back booths where she would demonstrate her manhood. Jerry didn't have a problem with her work. She probably had more of a problem with it than he did. However Jerry didn't like the risks involved with her hooking, and there were times when she got into trouble.

## Moving On

Ultimately it became clear that the relationship wouldn't mature into anything more serious. At that time, Jerry wasn't interested in marriage. Long before Jerry met Vanessa, he had been taking periodic trips to Thailand to alleviate his boredom. He first visited East Asia and later he travelled to Southeast Asia—including Bali, Thailand, Cambodia and Vietnam. Then he decided to move to Thailand. Of course the move ended their two-year relationship, not least because Vanessa wasn't a great letter-writer.

Vanessa died at the age of thirty-three. Jerry took her to hospital for dialysis treatment three times a week for six months. She drank heavily and had taken a lot of drugs when she was younger. Vanessa had a bleeding ulcer and her doctor told her to stop drinking alcohol, or she would die. So she quit drinking ... for six months. Every year there's a major international beauty contest of transsexuals in Hawaii. She was there with all of her friends, from all over Hawaii and America, and she said 'Oh, the hell with it, I'm gonna have a drink!' She had several. Two days later she was dead.

## SEX OPS IN THAILAND

Bangkok is a major sex-change capital of the world, as it is for other types of medical treatment. Bumrungrad International Hospital in Bangkok, one of thirty-three internationally accredited Thai hospitals, acquires over sixty per cent of its business from its 400,000 foreign patients each year. According to the Tourist Authority of Thailand (TAT), the other hospitals in Thailand draw around 800,000 foreign customers each year. Patients fly to Bangkok from all over the world to receive medical treatment, then take a week's vacation on the beach, and they still haven't spent what the surgery would have cost back home.

Bumrungrad Hospital charges in the region of US$3,000 for a breast augmentation operation, which requires up to two hours of surgery. Fees for other sex-change operations are displayed on the hospital's website (listed below).

Demand for sex-change operations is not just by men wanting to be women. Plastic surgery clinics have also experienced a sharp increase in female to male operations. According to USA Today, Yanhee Hospital carried out more SRS operations on women than men during 2006.

For several years after moving to Thailand, Jerry Hopkins would receive telephone calls from Hawaiian *mahus*—friends of Vanessa's— saying 'I'm coming to Bangkok for my sex change and I wondered whether you would visit the doctor with me?' So Jerry would meet them and 'hold their hand' throughout the sex reassignment process, including post-op recovery.

Jerry knew what type of bars the *mahus* wanted to visit and where they wanted to shop. Jerry provided a unique and specialized

215

type of medical tourism, for *katoey*. Vanessa's sisters always went to Dr Preecha Tiewtranon's plastic surgery clinic. Dr Preecha, who has over thirty years of experience in plastic surgery, is President of the Society of Plastic and Reconstructive Surgery in Thailand. He also founded the Preecha Aesthetic Institute (PAI).

In Jerry's book *Thailand Confidential* he reported on a sex change operation by Dr Preecha, which he personally witnessed. The story was published in *Metro Magazine*. Jerry also received permission from the manager of Casanova bar, Nana Plaza, to photograph the *katoey* in the bar one afternoon.

Kelly was the girl whose sex op he witnessed. She kept returning for different operations, like hip augmentation. On one occasion, Kelly arrived in Bangkok with a group of ten Hawaiian *mahus*. Three were having sex changes, another was having her hips operated on, and a couple came for breast surgery. Says Jerry 'It was just wonderful … it was like old times!' They all stayed in one big room at a hospital in east Bangkok until the end of their recuperation period.

Kelly phoned Jerry and told him they were in town. When Jerry visited them at the hospital, Kelly threw open the door. There she was, standing absolutely naked, looking like a picture in *Playboy*. She was stunning, completely passable as a woman. 'In Hawaii they call each other "fish", alluding to the smell of the pussy they don't have,' explains Jerry. 'You are "fish" when you're passable as a woman. A six-foot-tall Samoan *mahu* once said "I smell fish" when she saw Vanessa "Tuna straight from the can!"'

Jerry would take the girls who had come here for a sex-change operation to Casanova Bar to meet their Thai counterparts. 'It was hilarious and wonderful!' recalls Jerry. 'They'd all flock around, and soon everybody's dropping their tops and comparing boobs for flexibility and firmness. They would banter: "Where do you buy your underwear?" and "Do you have any problems with the cops?"'

For further information about medical services, including plastic surgery, at Bumrungrad International Hospital, refer to the website: *http://www.bumrungrad.com*. For further details about the Preecha Aesthetic Institute (PAI), refer to the following website: *http://www. pai.co.th*.

## THE LAW OF ATTRACTION

The Kinsey Reports represent two books on human sexual behavior: *Sexual Behavior in the Human Male* (1948) and *Sexual Behavior in the Human Female* (1953) by Dr. Alfred Kinsey and others. Kinsey was the founder of the Institute for Sex Research known as The Kinsey Institute, which is based at Indiana University.

Kinsey's research, which was controversial when published between 1948 and 1953, challenged conventional beliefs about sexuality and related taboo subjects. Kinsey reported on the prevalence of different sexual orientations to support his claim that ten per cent of the population is gay. Kinsey also asserted that sexuality can change over time, and that sexual behavior can be understood both as physical contact as well as purely psychological phenomena (desire, sexual attraction, fantasy).

Instead of just three categories of sexual identity (heterosexual, bisexual and homosexual), a seven-category system was adopted. The Kinsey sexuality rating scale measured sexual behavior from 0 to 6, with 0 being completely heterosexual and 6 completely homosexual.

A rank of 1 was considered predominantly heterosexual with only marginal homosexual tendency, a 2 mostly heterosexual and more than incidentally homosexual, a 3 equally homosexual and heterosexual, and so on. An additional category X was created for asexuals (those who experience no sexual desire).

The reports state that nearly 46% of the male subjects had 'reacted' sexually to persons of both sexes during the course of their adult lives, and 37% had at least one homosexual experience. 11.6% of white males (ages 20-35) were given a rating of 3 (equal heterosexual and homosexual experience/response) throughout their adult lives. The study also reported that 10% of American males surveyed were 'more or less exclusively homosexual for at least three years between the ages of 16 and 55' (in the 5 to 6 range).

Men attracted to *katoey* probably have a score somewhere in the middle of Kinsey's scale. They might meet *katoey* and be surprised to find themselves attracted to them. Then they have to face the choice between being influenced by societal norms, or testing uncharted forbidden pleasures.

Further information about The Kinsey Institute is available at the organization's website: *http://www.kinseyinstitute.org.*

## SUMMARY

- Thailand is a global centre for sex reassignment surgery (SRS);
- Most transsexuals are pre-operative (pre-op), which means they have a penis;
- Whereas most people are neither absolutely gay nor completely heterosexual, it is normal to be sexually identified somewhere between these two extremes;
- In Thailand, *katoey* are legally classified as men

and they have no rights as women;

- Transsexuals tend to have a small hypothalamus (part of their brain);
- *Katoey* have a reputation for providing the best oral sex.

# FINDING LOVE ONLINE

The internet has become a popular and socially accepted place for meeting romantic partners. An estimated one in five single Americans look for love online. Asians, too, are increasingly turning to the internet to take control of their love life.

Online love entrepreneurs are generating serious numbers. Match.com alone boasts fifteen million subscribers in thirty-seven countries, making it the biggest dating site in the world. They claim their dating website has resulted in over three million marriages and other long-term relationships.

Naturally the service favours foreign men seeking beautiful Asian ladies. There are up to six times more Asian women registered online than foreign men.

Many 'proper' Thai ladies use online meeting places because they have few alternative methods of meeting men. These girls rely on their family and friends for introductions, but these referrals often fail to impress them. By contrast, online dating systems enable empowered Thai ladies to be proactive and attract suitors instantly.

But beware, there are some Thai women looking for an economic association rather than true romance. Less fortunate Thai women see *farang* men as fabulously rich, with limitless economic resources. Word is out that marrying a *farang* man is a small price to pay for the elevated lifestyle and financial security on offer. Only by spending time with the ladies in person will a guy be able to fathom their real agenda.

The ease and convenience of online dating makes it an appealing alternative to traditional dating. Furthermore, the stigmas attached to online dating—namely that it is for lonely, desperate, or unattractive people—are history. Now many professional men and women are subscribing to dating websites.

A major advantage of online dating is the ability to garner contacts of beautiful Thai ladies before arriving in the Land of Smiles. It's possible to make a few online friends before reaching Bangkok's Suvarnabhumi airport.

## HOW IT WORKS

### Step 1: Compare Online Dating Sites

Your first step is to find at least one online dating site which suits you. You may choose to use an online search engine but be aware that the best marketed sites do not necessarily offer the best service.

### Step 2: Create Your Online Profile

Most online dating sites allow you to register free of charge, which enables you to complete your online personal profile. All you need is your own personal email address.

When creating your profile, you will be asked to provide a username to protect your real identity. Your profile will usually include biographical information plus a summary of the kind of partner and relationship you are looking for.

Inclusion of a photograph in the profile is usually optional. Some dating websites claim that profiles which include photographs generate at least three times as many messages. Most Asian ladies do not care about physical appearance, but more about financial security.

Completion of your personal profile may take up to twenty minutes. Carefully review the paid-membership services before spending any money. Usually email messaging and chat features are available only to paid members.

### Step 3: Search and Chat

This is the fun part: simply engage in friendly and flirtatious correspondence until you are both comfortable enough to meet in person. Many sites incorporate email, instant messaging, chat rooms and video chat, enabling you to get to know the person before arranging a meeting.

It's easy to maintain online relationships with several contacts consecutively using the same or different online dating sites.

### Step 4: Validation

One simple method of verifying the honesty of members is to ask questions relating to that person's profile. Check that her answers are consistent with the original profile.

Here is a posting about validation from the website forum at: *http://www.chinatravelguide.com*:

*I imagine it is less common for a Chinese woman to use dating sites than her Western counterparts. I have found that the (Chinese) women are generally divorced and in their forties. My sense of previous posts here and letters with friends is that Asian men are not interested in a 'discarded old woman' and seek young girls.*

*The key signs of scams are: the woman looks like a supermodel;*

*the woman does not respond to your questions; the woman asks for money; woman is registered in one country but lives in another.*

*So presuming that the woman looks only normally lovely; responds to your questions; doesn't ask you for money; and lives in the same country as her dating club membership ...*

*Examine the tone of her letters. Do they display any personal intimacy—or are they very business-like? Is she using a translator? Be wary of any translator's role in helping you to communicate. I have long suspected that they use the women who seek their help— charging them large sums of money. I do not know that first hand, but it is a grave suspicion.*

*There is one further concern with having translated love letters: you may have feelings for the translator and not the woman you are writing to. I am embarrassed to admit that I say this with first hand experience.*

*The language of love has a very small vocabulary. It works best for teenagers who don't usually have much to say. Spending several days with a woman you cannot speak with can become frustrating for both of you—even if you have strong feelings for each other. If you really like the woman and are comfortable that you are not being sucked into a scam, hire a translator to accompany you to lunch or the park (in this role, translators are fine).*

## WHO IS THIS FOR?

Thai women who use online dating websites are generally aged between eighteen and thirty-five. Many Thai women state explicitly that they are looking for an older Western man (usually forty to sixty years old) to 'take care' of them; the older men are considered more attentive, reliable and financially secure. The highest concentration of female members live in Bangkok and in the northeast of Thailand.

Romyen Kosaiyakanon, who completed a research project entitled *Cross-Border Marriages: A Case Study of Thai Women-Foreign Men Matches Through Online Dating Services in Thailand*, reports that many Thai women using online dating services are educated. She says a quarter of online registrants have a bachelor's degree and thirty per cent have a vocational degree'. She adds that half of the female members are divorced, and forty per cent claim to be single. According to the study, the average age of the Thai women who use online dating services is thirty-seven, with the youngest 18. The male members have an average age of fifty-three.

*Some ladies are looking for a rich guy, others are just having fun and a lot like to find serious relationship. The common rule is that women on dating websites are in control.* [Thaivisa.com forum]

The dating websites tend to draw ordinary women who are looking for a relationship with a Westerner. Some ladies have recently left school and seeking a more comfortable life. There are also many older women with university degrees and a steady job, who may be genuinely interested in romance with a *farang* man. Some of these women are too shy to seek foreign men any other way. There are also sex workers who use the website as a means of advertising their services.

*I met my wife on match.com. We have been together for over two years now, and we got married in July. There are many success stories from couples that have met on the net, and sadly, there are also stories of many rip-offs ... I can say that I would definitely rather get involved in a long term relationship with a girl from the internet rather than a bargirl.* [Thaivisa.com forum]

## THE GOOD NEWS

The following are some comments from satisfied customers, mainly from online forums. Gary comments on the CrossCultureLove.com forum:

*'These internet dating sites actually solve a huge logistics problem. How does a poor, decent Thai girl living in a tiny village meet a farang? It's not practical for her to drive the motorcycle 200Km round trip to 'hang around' at the mall in hopes of meeting someone. In my wife's village she observed that the few farang there seemed to treat their Thai wives well. She decided she wanted a farang husband. The only solution for her was to drive her motorcycle the 15Km to a small town that had an internet connection. She asked the owner's which website to join for meeting farang. They recommended ThaiLoveLinks.Com and the rest is history.*

*'So my experience has been a good one. Perhaps I've been lucky; who knows? My wife is lovely, very religious, hates bars/drinking/ drugs, is conservative with our money. She cooks, cleans, and takes good care of me. She reads, writes and speaks English well. She wanted to study at University but her family had little money so she had to work in the family business.'*

Several people provided positive comments about the ThaiLoveLinks.com dating website. Examples follow:

*'I found that ThaiLoveLinks (TLL) is a seriously run dating site. After 6 months (of using TLL) I found myself VERY close to getting married to a nice Thai lady! But long distance relationships are difficult. Eventually she changed her mind, but we're still friends.'*

*'I met my wife thru TLL [ThaiLoveLinks]. One year together and going strong. Actually there are a lot of really nice people on*

*TLL (along with a few of the usual scammers). You gotta be careful no matter where you meet someone; bar, internet, coffee shop, mall, it doesn't matter.*

'No sour grapes at all. I'm simply sharing my knowledge about these sites and telling people to be careful. I also have a couple of friends who had a wonderful experience with these sites, especially Thai Love Links.

'I've used ThaiLoveLinks. The service costs US$25 per month and I think it's great. Met some wonderful women, some who remain close friends to this day. Some never more than chatting, some I met for just one meal, some friendships. I've seen some of them get boyfriends, and one got married and moved to the US.

'I mostly filtered for college graduates and looked for people with good jobs. I'm 50+ and looked mostly for women in mid-30's with kids (don't need any biological time bombs going off). And I looked for women who live in Bangkok, where I live.

'I don't like going to bars to meet women, even pale-skinned hi-so (or whatever you want to call non-BG). I like having a chance to know someone online, chat and exchange photos, talk on the phone. If the vibe and info looks good, it's easy to arrange a dinner. I'd say 30% of the time, especially in the sub-30 year old women, they bring a friend along to the first date which is OK.'

## THE BAD NEWS

There are female predators using online dating sites specifically to extort as much money as possible from gullible foreign men.

Basil commented on a popular forum that the Thai women wanted to know where he worked, what his profession was, what kind of house he owned, what car he drove, and lastly, what he was like. He said it was like filling out a mortgage application form.

Similarly, there are also predatory men using online dating systems in order to get casual sex without having to pay for it. A cunning Israeli man—who believes strongly that only 'bad people' give money to women—concludes that online dating websites enable him to have sex with many beautiful young Thai ladies without paying them of a single baht.

The dating websites provide no sound method of quality control. All the websites offer are virtual meeting places, and anyone with an email address can join. Therefore it is easy to create a fictitious profile of a beautiful person, or enhance one's profile to attract more interest.

The most common method of falsifying profiles is to upload outdated photographs, or even images which have been visually enhanced using Photoshop software. According to Barry Sandal, author of the book *Foreign Relations*, most Thai ladies are truthful when they complete their online profiles; but they are more flexible with the truth when they chat.

Some dating websites require male members to pay for each item of correspondence in addition to a flat membership fee. Therefore it is possible to spend a lot of money without any guaranteed result.

## SCAMS

### Gary The Geezer's Scam

According to a Belgian website developer, a common scam involves a Western man, Gary The Geezer, who creates a dating website with many false profiles. Gary The Geezer (from Manchester) presents a portfolio of beautiful Thai women using stock photos and fictitious biographies. These imaginary profiles lure hundreds of excited men around the world, who send flirtatious messages in return. Gary The Geezer sends them an email alert stating that the beautiful lady has replied to them—they are in luck!—and her message will be forwarded as soon as they upgrade their account to a PAID membership. As soon as Gary the Geezer is notified of the cash receipt, he arranges for a freelance scribe to reply to the enthusiastic man who is already checking out flights to The Land of Smiles. Meanwhile Gary The Geezer is sitting on a barstool at his local tavern in Salford, downing his fourth pint of ale.

**Freelance Scribes**

Some Asian women who are registered with such websites have no intention of meeting Western men; they are paid by the website owners to write emails and encourage male members to become paid subscribers. These female scribes develop long-term relationships with male members but refuse to meet them in person.

**Other Online Scams**

There are even some reports of women using online dating services as con-artists; looking for men to sleep with, so they can walk away with the contents of his wallet.

There are several ways to be duped when using online dating sites, so be careful. Use the more reputable websites and be reluctant to pay anything other than a monthly or annual membership fee. For more about scams, refer to the chapter 'Popular Love Scams'.

## TIPS

The following tips will enable you to use Thai internet dating sites effectively and safely, without paying exorbitant fees:

### Research
Check out several dating websites and select the ones which suit your needs. Consider the company's services as well as the selection of female members listed. Also, make use of free trials to see what you like or don't like about a specific site before committing financially. Review the comments posted on popular forums—such as *www.crossculturelove.com*—about online dating websites.

### Read the Fine Print
Make sure you understand the company's policies and costs for each type of service; this will save money and get better results. Read the website's Terms & Conditions before you pay any money. Check whether the website owner will share your personal information with third party companies, because this practice can lead to unwelcome spam and even fraud.

### Maintain Privacy
Don't give out personal information such as full name, address, or phone number to just anyone who asks for it. Make sure you have a comfortable level of trust in a person before sharing such details.

### Be patient
While it can save time and offer quick results, online dating still takes patience and persistence. Your dream girl is unlikely to write you a

message as soon as you sign up, so be willing to wait and spend time browsing through profiles.

## Be Polite

It's ok to have fun and be flirtatious, but don't be rude or 'talk dirty'. The following comments were posted on the *Thaivisa.com* discussion forum:

*If you are looking for first date sex I don't think this is the best place to look, but it has happened to me. There are some women happy to just have a friend for movie or dinner—maybe things get more intimate over time. Same as any dating in Thailand once you've had your first dates. And some are really hardcore to find a serious relationship. Just depends on what you are looking for.*

*I can tell you from talking to a bunch of these women that they HATE men who get online and talk dirty and think this is some kind of BG service and chat room. Too many men think that Thai women are just sitting online waiting for sexy chat or some bloke who expects to have someone meet him at the airport and straight to the hotel based on a 5 min. chat. These are in my experience 100% sincere nice women looking for a man to date, marry, whatever—But not for quick sex and money.*

## Verify her Authenticity

Obviously, you want to know that the woman you're getting involved with is indeed a real woman who is also interested in meeting you. Video chat is a good way to see, in real time, the person you are messaging. Don't hesitate to ask for information such as birthday and measurements to double check against her profile.

## Slowly, Slowly

While it is possible to build the foundation of a relationship online, personal encounters are certainly necessary to take things to the next level. Try not to get too serious with a person you've never met face to face.

## Meet in a public place

If you are ready to meet a woman in person, be smart about it. She may turn out to be nothing like the person you 'got to know' online. For the first encounter, be sure to meet in a public place. This is in order to avoid any possibility of violence or robbery, however unlikely it may be.

## Too good to be true?

Keep in mind that there is always a possibility that the woman you've met online is only interested in you so that she can enjoy the benefits of your economic generosity. Be wary of the young and beautiful women who sounds too good to be true—because that could indeed be the case.

Case Study

In the Northeast province of Issan, there are several internet cafés which offer matchmaking services for local women looking for *farang* husbands. Many Issan women dream of being swept away by a *farang* Prince Charming. Mrs Nongkhai is a Love Entrepreneur offering cyber-matchmaking services for a flat fee of US$150, plus an additional fee after the couple agrees marriage.

In Ubon Ratchathani, a female school teacher was killed by someone she met online. Caution should be exercised by all cyber-chatters. Here are Mrs Nongkhai's guidelines for online chatting:

- Don't trust anyone who doesn't use a webcam;
- Define your acceptable boundaries of communication at the beginning (for example, no swear words);
- Don't meet anyone within say 3 month's of meeting online;
- Always meet cyber friends in public places initially; notify a friend of your whereabouts during the date.

## POPULAR SITES

The following table shows some of the bigger Thai internet dating services, but is by no means a comprehensive list. It is worth the effort to get online and check out a number of sites before making a decision.

| WEBSITE ADDRESS | FEES | FEATURES | OTHER INFO |
|---|---|---|---|
| www. thailovelinks.com | $25 per month with discounts for longer subscriptions | Video chat, voicemail, message translation | The largest Thai dating website |
| http:// th.match.com | $20 per month, cheaper for 6- or 12-month subscribers | Advanced 'chemistry' matching | Thai division of the popular Match.com |
| www. thailove.com | Free | Email and chat | High 4:3 male-female ratio |
| www. mythaicupid.com | $8 per month | Video chat, Thai language section | 7 day free trial with all features enabled |

## Other Dating Websites

The following are some other popular online dating websites:

- AsiaFriendFinder (*http://www.asiafriendfinder.com*) has 6.7 million members;
- SweetSingles (*http://www.sweetsingles.com*) is a Thai website which appears to have many fake profiles;
- DatingThailand (*http://www.datingthailand.com*) offers free basic membership with many genuine-looking women;
- MyThaiCupid (*http://www.mythaicupid.com*);
- Thailand Friends (*http://www.thailandfriends.com*);
- Thai Mate (*http://www.thaimate.com*);
- Adult Friend Finder (*http://www.adultfriendfinder.com*);
- Friendster (*http://www.friendster.com*).

Online chat-rooms are also popular meeting places. Examples

include:

- *myspace.com*;
- *hi5.com*;
- *camfrog.com.*

## SUMMARY

- Most internet dating sites provide minimal quality control so it's your responsibility to validate the authenticity of your new friends;
- While many foreigners have established serious relationships with Asian ladies via online dating sites, some people have been conned, so be careful;
- Meeting online is particularly appealing for busy people who do not want to look for their prospective partner in expat bars or clubs.

# CROSS-CULTURE GAY RELATIONSHIPS

*Thai gays tend to be internet savvy, so the best place to meet gay partners in Thailand is in cyberspace*

PHIL NICKS

Thailand is one of the most well known gay-friendly countries, partly due to the tolerance of gays in society. Thais often speak openly about the three sexes: male, female and *katoey* (usually referred to as cross-dressers or transvestites). Another reason for the tolerance of gays in Thailand is the prevalence of Buddhist philosophy which is free of religious dogma. Buddhist gays are not 'locked up in a closet' unlike many of their western counterparts.

Gays are tolerated in Thai society but they are often discriminated against. Gays in Thailand usually have challenging social lives, and can have difficulty finding true love. According to Buddhism, the suffering that gays experience is a lesson for misdeeds committed in previous lives.

Thais are open about gender issues. The first questions you will be asked are: 'Are you married? ... No, then do you have a girlfriend? ... No? ... Then do you have a boyfriend?' This same dialog occurs whenever you meet a new person—anywhere.

Thailand is famous for its liberal 'entertainment' industry which includes both gay and trans-gender components, although gay enterprises maintain a lower profile. Today, Thailand's entertainment industry encompasses a plethora of gay establishments catering to gay tourists and foreign residents who consider themselves as straight. It is not unusual for heterosexual married men, who have conventional lifestyles in their home country, to visit Thailand without their wives or children, to navigate the gay scene.

Thailand has much more to offer gays than Western countries. The key difference is that gays can live life more openly as a homosexual than in their home country. Lesbian couples also exist in Thailand, but they receive less media attention than gays, although this is changing.

## TYPES OF CROSS-CULTURE GAY RELATIONSHIPS

Any type of gay relationship is possible in Thailand. Every harmonious cross-culture relationship is based upon a mutually agreed 'deal'. You can arrange any type of relationship contract you want as long as you respect each other.

The main types of gay relationships are listed below. This list is not exhaustive and it's also possible to combine these common relationship arrangements. For example, it is common for gays to combine long-term relationships with casual encounters.

### Long-Term Gay Relationships

In long-term relationships the two men consider themselves a couple. The couple is in the relationship for the long term, similar to a heterosexual marriage. They probably live together and go out together as any normal couple would do.

## One Night Stands

One night stands, or brief encounters, are an important aspect of the gay scene.

Two guys meet and spend the night together. They both have fun. After their encounter they have no responsibility for each other's welfare. There is no emotional attachment, just fun (*sanuk*).

One night stands are more common in the gay community than amongst heterosexuals for several reasons. Many men are in various stages of acknowledging their sexual identity and brief encounters are a means to self-knowledge. Most gays are not aware of their sexuality at first, so they think they are straight but 'gay-curious'. Later, after several one night stands, they accept that they are primarily gay or bisexual.

Many men who consider themselves heterosexual enjoy one night stands with gays because they do not want to form a gay relationship in public. Other men may believe they are gay but they prefer to appear as heterosexual in public.

## Pay-As-You-Go (PAYG) Relationships

PAYG relationships in Thailand are usually short-time encounters between Western men and bar boys (male Thai sex workers). This arrangement works in a similar way to the heterosexual male meeting a female bargirl (female sex worker). The relationship may last one night or the duration of the foreigner's stay in Thailand.

Sometimes PAYG encounters continue as a distance relationship after the foreigner leaves the country. It may or may not be clear from the beginning that the Thai man expects periodic remuneration by way of money or goods purchased for him. The *farang* may remit a monthly retainer of around US$1,000 in return for exclusive attention whenever he is in Southeast Asia.

The male Thai sex worker may not be gay; instead he may be a heterosexual male working for gays to earn a living. Furthermore, the Western male may be living a straight life in his home country, and only interested in trying something different in Thailand, so both parties are self-identified heterosexuals engaging in gay behavior.

## Relationships with Retirees

Relationships between young Thai men and Western retirees are common in Thailand. In Thailand retired men can have gay relationships with young men who are a small fraction of their age—typically thirty years younger—without criticism from the lay public.

Western gays emphasize the importance of age compatibility; so many older gays are excluded from gay social networks. Therefore it is extremely difficult for an old Western gay male to find a young partner in his home country. In Thailand older men are seen by young Thai gays as rich in both experience and wealth, so they are considered goldmines.

## Multiple Relationships

Multiple relationships are arrangements in which one or both men in a relationship have a relationship (or encounters) with other men or women. The Western man may have a relationship—possibly with a legal wife—in his home country, or he is promiscuous in Thailand. Alternatively, the Thai man may have a Thai wife, girlfriend or other boyfriends.

Extra-relationship encounters may be mutually agreed between both parties; or the casual relationships may be kept a secret to one or both parties. For example, the Thai man may know that the Western man has a wife in the home country, and the wife would probably not know about the boyfriend in Thailand.

## GAY MEETING PLACES

### Meeting Online

There are two main ways to meet someone in Thailand: online and in person. The internet is a practical medium for foreigners wanting to meet gays in Thailand when they visit the country on holiday. Now the internet can be used as an instant meeting place, allowing users to 'meet' online just minutes before agreeing physical contact.

There are several gay dating websites, such as gay.com, which allow members to find suitable partners anywhere. The quantum leap from internet chat to personal meeting can be just minutes apart. The trend is internet interaction replacing face-to-face introductions in bars and clubs. Many people nowadays regard the pursuit of 'picking up' partners in a bar scenario as sleazy.

Most young gays in Thailand understand the benefits of meeting online—it's cheaper (because you don't have to buy drinks at a bar) and it's easier to filter unwelcome approaches (eliminating annoying conversations with irritating people).

### Meeting in Person

As convenient as the internet is, there is no substitute for meeting in person. In Thailand, you can meet gays anywhere—or rather, they can meet you anywhere! Since Thai gays tend to be more confident than their western counterparts, they are more likely to be openly gay. This means they are not as shy about asking a man if he is gay. Thai gays show interest in other men in every imaginable place:

travel shops, restaurants, bars, clubs, airline check-in counters, and even immigration check points!

In Thailand, gays meet in bars, clubs, restaurants, and at gay events. Any gay *farang* should check out Bangkok's gay entertainment scene in the Silom area (Sois 2 and 4, and Soi Cowboy); this noteworthy gay district even draws heterosexual couples, curious to investigate the gay scene in Thailand.

The following table lists several popular gay or gay-friendly venues:

| NAME | TYPE | LOCATION | DESCRIPTION |
|------|------|----------|-------------|
| Purple Dragon | Travel Agency | Bangkok | This is possibly the oldest gay travel company in Bangkok. Specializing in travel in Southeast Asia. |
| The Balcony | Pub | Silom, Soi 4, Bangkok | A long-standing favourite of Bangkok. Outside terrace as well as inside seating. Always full. |
| DJ Station | Disco | Silom, Soi 2, Bangkok | Disco featuring cabaret on weekends. Several levels of dancing with gallery views. |
| Darling Wine Bar | Bar | Huay Keaw, Chiang Mai | Small and quiet wine bar. |
| Sparoma | Sauna | Padad Road, Chiang Mai | Well-established sauna located just outside the city along the Ping River. |
| Bubbles | Disco | Porn Ping Hotel, Chiang Mai | Modern disco often packed with Thais and tourists. |

For additional places in Bangkok, or for other cities, refer to the above websites.

## DATING ETIQUETTE

Thailand, despite being tolerant with gays, is not so tolerant about public displays of affection. Compared to the West, Thailand is very conservative about expressing feelings. Gay or straight, kissing and hugging in public is not acceptable in most situations. Even holding hands may cause disapproving glances.

In tourist hot-spots where Thais are accustomed to foreign behavior, they tolerate acts of affection in public, but it is still not accepted. When dating a Thai you should be careful not to embarrass your partner. Let your partner take the initiative on what's appropriate and follow his lead.

Thais have great respect for those who are older than themselves. This praise also translates into more responsibility. While dating, the older person (or the person with the larger wallet) is expected to take care of the bill. Foreigners are widely considered in Thailand to be rich and therefore are often expected to take care of the bills. Splitting the bills for anything is uncommon.

## LEGAL STATUS

In cross-cultural gay relationships in Thailand, there is no official civil union, which means that gay relationships are not legally recognized. This means that foreigners are unable to obtain a 'marriage visa' or fiancé visa to stay with their Thai partner in Thailand. There are also no tax benefits available for gay couples.

Although foreigners can live in Thailand long term, they cannot become Thai citizens or vote in elections. Also restrictions are placed on foreigners owning property; so gay couples usually register land in the Thai man's name.

Thailand has been updating its laws relating to gays. Up until 2002, according to Thai law, homosexuality was regarded as a mental disorder. Since 2005, gays and transsexuals have been allowed to join the armed forces.

According to Peter Jackson, a researcher specializing in Thai gay issues, 'The previous political regime of Prime Minister Thaksin Shinawatra had conservative moral policies, and gay magazines and other gay businesses were often raided. Somewhat ironically, since the military coup that overthrew Thaksin in September 2006, the climate for homosexual people has improved markedly. There's been a boom in gay businesses, including new gay magazines,' (15 December 2007, *Financial Times Online, http://www.ft.com/cms/*).

In 2007, the Military Junta ruling Thailand incorporated gender issues into their new constitution. 'The Thai government's Constitutional Drafting Assembly (CDA) adopted language to ensure equal rights for gays, lesbians and trans-gendered people on Thursday, June 29th [2007]. The draft constitution expressly refers to people of 'other sexual identities' which includes trans-gendered *katoey* as well as gay men and lesbians' (02 July 2007, Thai Constitution to Protect Gays, Dreaded Ned's online: *http://www.dreadedned.com/ news/2/110/*).

## Case Study: Money Matters

Sanchai and Dave met in a disco in Bangkok. Dave was new to Thailand and also to the Thai gay scene. After several drinks, he began to lose his inhibitions and started dancing with various guys. Towards the end of the night, he chatted with one of these guys called Sanchai. Sanchai was a good looking guy in his mid-twenties, a good dancer, and an even better conversationalist. He spoke English well. After the final songs were played, Dave and Sanchai left and spent the night together.

The next morning, Dave had to travel back to Bangkok to work. Sanchai suggested accompanying him since he had no imminent commitments. Dave, who was enjoying his company, decided that Sanchai should join him for a few more days. The days passed quickly, with Dave working during the day at a local school and Sanchai staying in Dave's room watching TV.

When Sanchai had to return home after five days together, Dave was thinking that their time together could be the start of a good friendship and possibly a relationship. He liked Sanchai because he was intelligent, easy to talk to, and had a relaxing effect on Dave. Before Sanchai left Dave's apartment. he asked him for some money to cover his travel expenses.

Dave handed out a 1,000 baht note without thinking about it. After all, Dave wanted to continue the relationship and he wanted to help him. Sanchai immediately protested about the meager payment and demanded more. Thais rarely show anger in public, so Dave was quite shocked.

Dave thought that Sanchai was a genuinely nice person and wanted to meet him again. They had enjoyed their time together and there had been no discussion about money. Sadly, Sanchai viewed the previous five days as work, for which he needed a reasonable salary. He said he could have earned much more money by visiting the local nightclub where he met Dave.

In Thailand it is difficult to define a sex worker because many 'freelancers' make a living by meeting foreigners in bars and nightclubs, like Sanchai. Dave thought they were real friends but Sanchai had a completely different agenda.

### Case Study: Not Everyone is 'Out' in Thailand

Tee and Robert met via the internet. Tee, who was gay, was not 'out' to his family. Many of his friends knew about his gay lifestyle, though he never openly discussed his sexual identity with anyone.

Robert and Tee agreed to meet for coffee. They got on well together so they started dating regularly. Eventually, Tee invited Robert out with his friends. Everyone but Tee's family knew that they had formed a relationship together. Nobody was at all awkward about being in the company of two gay men. However, Tee didn't want to tell his parents about his lifestyle.

In Thailand, where gays are tolerated, some Thais are still very conscious of the effect of their actions on their family. This reflects the Thai concept of 'kreng jai', or consideration for others. Tee was aware that although his family would never be confronted in a negative way about his sexual identity, they would feel embarrassed and possibly disappointed.

## TOMS AND DEES

Thailand has a thriving lesbian community, although it is not 'in your face'. Thailand is much better known for its 'out' gay community than its lesbian community, although they probably exist in similar numbers. Thai lesbians do not use the term 'lesbian' as they associate the word with pornography; instead they prefer to call themselves Toms (as in tomboys) and Dees (as in ladies). Toms are more masculine and Dees are feminine.

Unlike the male gay community, toms and dees don't have specific 'lesbian venues' that they visit. Most toms and dees visit gay bars, restaurants, discos and regular heterosexual venues.

There is very little interaction between lesbians and gays in Thailand. Many Thai gays act cold towards lesbians.

Information about lesbian venues is tabulated in the following table:

| WEBSITE | INTERNET ADDRESS | DESCRIPTION |
|---------|------------------|-------------|
| Lesla | www.lesla.com/eng.htm | This website offers news, chat, webboards and other information including photos as well as an online shop. |
| Bkkles | www.bangkoklesbian.com/ | This website has a nice section about where to go, a section for tourists, as well as the standard news, forum, and chat for social networking. |

## GAY RESOURCES

**Books For Gays**

- *The Intrinsic Quality of Skin*, Floating Lotus Publications
- *Dear Uncle Go: Male Homosexuality in Thailand*, Floating Lotus Publications
- *Thai conversation for Gay Tourists*, Saksit Pakdeesiam
- *Thai for Gay Tourists*, Paiboon Publishing

**Internet Resources**

The use of the internet in planning gay travel or meeting other single gays is essential. Most websites tend to be in English language and may not be Thai focused, but are used by Thais to meet foreigners.

The Spartacus International Gay Travel Guide (see SPARTACUS International Gay Guide 2007, 36th edition *http://www. spartacusworld.com/gayguide/*).

The internet is the most popular way to enter gay Thailand. The following table summarizes several major gay websites:

| WEBSITE | INTERNET ADDRESS | DESCRIPTION |
|---------|------------------|-------------|
| Gay.com | www.gay.com | This is a global gay dating network where gays can create profiles and view those created by others. Not a strictly Thai website, you can search for people anywhere in the world and reply with gay.com's email or chat directly with the built-in chat program. |

| Utopia Asia | www.utopia-asia.com/tipsthai.htm | This travel website is good for finding gay events, accommodation, bars and restaurants. They also provide links to other gay organizations. |
|---|---|---|
| Dragoncastle | http://dragoncastle.net/ | This website specializes in gay services, from dating and forums to travel. There are also photo galleries. |
| Dreaded Ned's | www.dreadedned.com/ | Another guide offering information by city and venue along with news and personals sections. |

Other popular online gay meeting places include:

- *http://www.gaydar.co.uk*
- *http://www.guys4men.com*
- *http://www.gthai.net*

## *KATOEY* SCENE

For a definition of *katoey*, the third sex, refer to the chapter 'Gender Illusionists'.

The *katoey* community is well integrated into the gay scene in Thailand. For example many gay Thai men enjoy watching *katoey* beauty pageants and cabaret shows.

*Katoey* are not to be confused with gay Thai men; *katoey* do not want to be considered gay (since they feel female already and are attracted to the opposite sex), nor do gays want to be considered *katoey* (because gay Thai men feel they are men attracted to the same sex, even if they are effeminate).

## TIPS

Let your partner guide you through the labyrinth of social customs.

## SUMMARY

- The gay scene in Thailand is highly developed and offers myriad opportunities for homosexual foreigners;
- Thai society is tolerant of gays but not completely accepting of them;
- Many Thai sex workers who service gay customers are heterosexual;
- If you meet a gay friend in a nightclub and have fun for a few days, don't be surprised if you receive a 'bill' before you go back home.

# ILLUMINATED RELATIONSHIPS

*All the best medicines and good food in the world cannot help one achieve longevity unless one knows and practices the Tao of Yin and Yang*

KO HUNG, TAOIST PHYSICIAN

*Romantics play with illusion like fire, and usually end up burnt to a cinder*

PHIL NICKS

Where can we find illuminated (or spiritual) cross-culture relationships? The monk, called Rocky (because he looked like a shaven Sylvester Stalone), smiled when he heard this question. Then he explained that it's only possible to have an illuminated relationship with oneself—not with another person.

Rocky said that monks are not allowed relationships with other people, even their own family. They are certainly not permitted to have sexual relations with anyone. The Lord Buddha released himself from all emotional attachments, including his wife and family.

The concept of a spiritual relationship with a sexual partner is a contraction of terms. The cause of pain and suffering is emotional attachment and unfulfilled sensory desire.

For minimal emotional attachment in a relationship it's better to contract for a short time only. For example, enjoy a massage and then let go of the feeling. Partnerships inevitably develop emotional attachment as the relationship develops. Another fact is that most mutually beneficial exchange of knowledge in a relationship occurs during the initial hours of contact.

The ancient Chinese Taoist philosophers provide a wealth of knowledge about how to live healthy spiritual relationships. There are several Taoist masters living in Asia, including Mantak Chia, who teaches how to cultivate male and female energy.

Mantak Chia has written many books about spiritual development and natural health, including *Multiorgasmic Woman*; and he founded a natural health spa and resort called Tao Gardens, near Chiang Mai in Northern Thailand. The website address of Tao Gardens is *http://www.tao-garden.com*.

## WHAT IS AN ILLUMINATED RELATIONSHIP?

The prerequisite for an illuminated cross-culture relationship is two people from different cultures who are both independently happy with their lives. Both partners must be able to sustain a fulfilling life on their own before they can enjoy an illuminated relationship together.

The illuminated couple is attracted to each other for positive reasons, rather than fear of being alone or financially insecure. Relationships based upon fear are usually codependent arrangements; typically, one partner fears being alone and the other fears poverty.

The couple trusts and respects each other; they do not depend on each other. The couple offers unconditional love for one another, so they do not try to control or manipulate their partners.

## Congruent Goals

Illuminated couples have common goals and support each other to reach their highest ambitions. This works best when both parties rank personal (and spiritual) development as a high priority in their lives. The basis of personal development (or evolutionary transformation) is enhanced wellbeing and unity. So illuminated relationships are uplifting!

Social philosopher, Dr Pravese, who lectures at Mahidol University in Bangkok, advocates an index of wellbeing (known at Gross Domestic Happiness, abbreviated as GDH), instead of the economic indicator, Gross Domestic Product (GDP). The index of real progress measures the mood (or emotional frequency) of the population. Happy people are evolved people.

One major test of an illuminated relationship is when your partner gets an opportunity of advancement which conflicts with your personal comfort. For example, can you let go of your partner, even if it's best for him or her?

## Trust

Each partner trusts each other. Without trust the relationship falls apart (so if you think you need to hire a private detective to follow your wife, you don't really need your spouse). A prevalent issue in Thai–*farang* relationships is jealousy; this indicates insecurity and a desire to control the other person.

## Acceptance

The couple accepts each other for who they really are; neither partner needs to try to change or manipulate the other person to suit their own selfish agendas. The couple does not have any unrealistic expectations of each other, and neither do they make any assumptions about them. Many problems in cross-culture relationships stem from unrealistic assumptions and expectations of each other.

In illuminated relationships, love is unconditional; so we love each other regardless of what our partner does. The love is pure, without any 'ifs' or 'buts'.

### Synergy

A synergetic relationship benefits both parties because the union creates more value than the two parties could achieve independently. Mathematically, the sum of one plus one in synergetic relationships would exceed the number, two.

### Non-Attachment

Illuminated relationships are between happy people, not 'needy' or insecure people. Needy or vulnerable people are prone to emotional attachment in relationships; these relationships are dysfunctional and unhealthy. So if you want an illuminated relationship, find happiness in yourself before attracting another happy person.

### Respect

Mutual respect is essential in illuminated relationships, as is compassion. In a balanced relationship neither partner looks up nor down on their partner.

### Commitment

The partners are committed to their relationship contract, which they review and evaluate periodically. The couple is also committed to each other's personal development, and therefore to resolving any issues or disputes. Each resolved issue brings the relationship to a higher level.

Intimacy and the ability to acknowledge and discuss sensitive or awkward subjects are keys to illuminated relationships. A major problem in many Thai–*farang* relationships is denial; it is considered impolite to hurt another person's feelings, even if the purpose is to overcome a problem.

### Reality

The foundations of illuminated relationships are truthfulness (even when it hurts your partner), open communication and direct honest negotiation (rather than being indirect). Conversely, the great musician, Frank Zappa, commented about fairytale romances in a song entitled 'Romance is for Arseholes'. Romantics play with illusion like fire, and usually end up burnt to a cinder.

### Passion

Illuminated relationships tend to be driven by passion. Orthodox structures, such as the institution of marriage, favour social status and security, and usually kill the passion and excitement of unregulated relationship adventures. It has been scientifically proven that the rate of sexual intercourse drops dramatically after a couple marries.

Another issue related to regulated relationships is the couple's tendency to live in the past and the future, instead of the present. Plans and expectations are part of the marriage package, along with insurance and other tools for reducing risk. If passionate relationships are fizzy, marriages tend to be 'flat'.

### Equality

The power in the illuminated relationship is balanced. Joint decisions are negotiated and really agreed by the couple; and neither party holds economic power over the other. Either both parties are independently financially secure, or there are no economic boundaries within the relationship.

## TANTRA

Tantric sex is an enlightened form of sexual experience, focusing on the quality rather than quantity of the actions.

Tantra, which mean 'woven together' in Sanskrit, is a yogic practice of sexual union between man and woman. There are several types of tantra, including the Kundalini way and Tibetan Buddhism and pre-Buddhist Bon forms of tantra.

Most teachers of tantra advocate seminal retention as a prerequisite for spiritual advancement. Taoist sexual alchemy teaches sexual practices as a way to promote health and longevity; whereas Tibetan Buddhism and pre-Buddhist Bon tantra combine pre-Buddhist goddess worship with ancient Tibetan animism known as Bon.

The Taoist master, Mantak Chia, teaches how to control and harness male and female sexual energy. The Taoist philosophy is for sex to be the servant, not the master. Traditionally, people who are indoctrinated by religion allow themselves to be sexually repressed, causing sex to become their master.

In many contemporary tantric practices, sexual intercourse is a minor part of the experience, and sometimes it is completely dispensed with. Awareness and quality of the sensuous experience is the main goal.

# INTER-DEPENDENCE

Healthy relationships are free of dependence. Most human beings are somewhat dependent upon others, at least inter-dependent (or working together for a common purpose).

Co-dependent relationships are the norm, particularly in marriage contracts. In many standard Thai–*farang* relationships, the foreigner provides the financial security and their partner 'takes care' of them. The Thai offers a service unimaginable in *Farang*land, so the foreigner is being opportunistic and engaging in 'relationship arbitrage'.

Usually the *farang* men develop emotional attachment to their Asian lady much sooner than she does. These ladies need to be practical and realistic in order to survive in a polygamous environment. She will not attach emotionally to her mate until he has demonstrated his commitment to her financially. Each time economic power is transferred to her, her emotions run deeper.

Therefore, the *farang* must be reasonable generous for his cross-culture relationship to work effectively. If the Thai senses that his or her partner is ki neaw (which literally means 'sticky shit') or unable to share their resources, they will not commit to the relationship.

There are voluntary groups for co-dependents—known as CODA—all over the world. These groups exist in Thailand, though Thais rarely attend the meetings (partly because of the potential loss of face). The worldwide website of CODA is *http://www.codependents. org*.

The *farang* women married to Thais tend to be controlling people (and like to organize and mollycoddle their young partners). The *farang* men, on the other hand, tend to be lonely and vulnerable to addictions, especially alcoholism and sex addiction.

## HEALTHY RELATIONSHIPS

There is a popular misconception that healthy relationships are easy and always harmonious. In fact, healthy relationships can be quite challenging, especially if both parties are assertive and willful.

Without sufficient fluency in a common language (usually Thai or English) it's almost impossible to resolve relationship issues, and therefore progress as a couple. Consider also, that in Thai culture it is considered impolite to confront, criticize, object or hurt another person's feelings; this can act as a cultural roadblock to the relationship's progress.

A vital key to every healthy relationship is, of course, trust. Now, it's extremely difficult for Thais to trust one another because infidelity is an accepted societal norm. Jealousy and unreasonable demands on their partner's attentiveness are major obstacles in Thai–*farang* relationships. Some people describe their Thai lady friends as 'insanely jealous.'

Ideally both parties to the relationship have common life goals. A common bone of contention for *farang* is the importance of their partner's family. A Thai person's primary duty is to support her family, including parents and offspring from a previous marriage and siblings). Taking care of their partner is of secondary importance. Foreigners who expect exclusive attention get frustrated quickly.

## HEALTHY BEDROOM PURSUITS

### Love vs Sex

A shamanic practitioner based in Chiang Mai said that the root of all problems in the world arise from conception based on the pursuit of sexual pleasure (without love). If everyone had sex based on real love, their offspring would be truly content. There would be no lonely or insecure people, and no resulting addictive behaviour.

Some *farang* living in Thailand are products of dysfunctional families. If they are completely happy with their family and culture, why would they uproot their place of residence? The aforementioned shamanic practitioner believes the type of addictive behaviour prevalent amongst Thailand's expatriates indicates deep loneliness associated with conception without real love between their parents.

## Taoist Bedroom Arts

The principles of Taoism were established in China by Lao Tze in the Tao Teh Ching about 5,000 years ago. Traditional Chinese culture progressed according to the wisdom of the old sages who developed Taoism, the universal and enduring way of nature.

A young boy called Jack, from the north of England, was teased at school for being perpetually late. His bullies would ridicule him in a thick Yorkshire accent 'Eeh, Jack, you're late!' Taoist philosophy goes a step further by advocating abstinence from ejaculation.

Chinese people do not delineate sex between the sacred (within matrimony) and profane (outside marriage), unlike the Christian tradition. There is no sense of guilt about sex as there is in western countries. There are, however, clear distinctions between healthy and unhealthy sexual habits.

According to Wu Hsien 'The male belongs to Yang. Yang's nature is such that the male is easily aroused but also quick to retreat. The female belongs to Yin. Yin's nature is such that the female is slow to be aroused and also slow to be satiated.'

Taoist sex requires the man to prevent ejaculation, saving his semen in order to conserve his energy. The woman, in turn, enjoys complete sexual pleasure in exchange for her health-promoting energy. 'The retention of semen is highly beneficial to man's health.' [Su Nu Ching]

Absolute celibacy can be as harmful as undisciplined sexual activity. The aim of Taoist sexual activity is to transmute sexual energy into pure spiritual power. This is made possible when the man suppresses his emissions, absorbing the woman's fluids, enabling his semen to return to his brain, thereby promoting longevity.

The Chinese philosophers conducted sexual research into fang-shu ('bedroom arts') and published illustrated texts known as 'pillow books' for each bride and groom's wedding ceremony from the third century BC onwards. Unlike India's Karmasutra, the Chinese pillow books focus on enabling sexual activity to benefit health and longevity as well as enhancing sexual pleasure.

## Sexual Gluttony

Many people in Thailand overindulge in sex. *Farang* men arriving in the Land of Smiles tend to go berserk when they see such alluring feminine creatures everywhere. After years of gender conflict and being trampled over by surly uptight feminists, it's an awesome lifestyle change for many guys.

Over-eating, drinking alcohol, and inactivity each increase sexual desire, but inhibit sexual performance. Animal products, including meat, eggs and cheese, stimulate sexual desire but also impede sexual performance. The result is many overweight 'sexpats' seeking solace in a Viagra pill which is a further risk to their health.

Dr Edwin Flatto, in his cautionary book *WARNING: Sex may be hazardous to your health* says that a vegetarian diet reduces sexual desire and enhances sexual performance. He recommends limiting sexual activity to enhance health and longevity.

Dr Flatto was asked by one of his female patients what he ate for protein. 'Nuts and seeds,' he replied. Then he asked her about her source of protein. 'Seminal fluid,' she replied frankly. 'It's a complete protein and has all the best elements and proteins necessary to nourish my body.'

## EASTERN CHAKRA THEORY

According to ancient Eastern wisdom, there are seven primary energy centres in the human being, known as chakras. Each chakra has a specific energetic function.

| CHAKRA NUMBER | NAME OF CHAKRA | PURPOSE OF CHAKRA |
|---|---|---|
| First | Root Chakra | Physical Survival |
| Second | Sacral | Creativity & Sex |
| Third | Solar Plexus | Ego & Willpower |
| Forth | Heart | Emotions |
| Fifth | Throat | Self-Expression |
| Sixth | Third Eye | Intuition |
| Seventh | Crown | Spirituality |

When a person's chakra is open, their energy flows normally, but when the energy centre is closed, there is an energy blockage which causes disease. A perfectly healthy person has all seven chakras open. A person who is broken-hearted is likely to have a closed heart chakra, whereas a charismatic person is likely to have a strong open solar plexus chakra.

In relationships, our chakras determine who we attract. Few people are strong in each level; some people are more spiritually developed than others; whereas others are more physically developed. Therefore we can resonate energetically with different people on varying levels.

Soul mates resonate on the higher levels whereas 'sex buddies' resonate on the second chakra level. In Thailand, many people have open sacral chakras, and are accordingly receptive to sensuous experiences. The monks usually have strong open third eye and crown chakras. So if you want an illuminated relationship, give your chakras an energetic tune-up.

## ENLIGHTENED COUPLES

The best test of ascertaining whether a couple is enlightened is to establish whether they are really a couple. If they are a couple, then they cannot be enlightened.

### The Missionaries

Thailand hosts hundreds of missionaries from all over the world. One of the Ten Commandments is 'Thou shalt not commit adultery'; and every good Christian tries to obey God's rulebook lest they be purged for their mortal sins.

David Smith, a British missionary working in Northern Thailand had an affair with another man's wife called Shiela. Shiela says that David refused to have sexual intercourse with her; however during the four year relationship he regularly enjoyed mutual masturbation with her. Sheila commented that he always said 'Thank you!' when he was finished.

The moral of this story is that some Christians have identified a 'loophole' in the Ten Commandments. Whereas having sex with another man's wife constitutes adultery, mutual masturbation is just being friendly. And anyway, it's OK as long as you are polite and say 'Thank you!' afterwards.

## The New Age Couple

Ralph Bradley and his Thai wife, Lah, teach yoga in the north of Thailand. The couple is immersed in the New Age world of fasting, herbal teas, detox, colon hydrotherapy, meditation and incense.

Ralph usually takes an annual pilgrimage to India to hone his yoga techniques at an ashram. The trip doubles up as professional development training course and holiday. Last year Lah went to India to study yoga instead of Ralph. So here is an empowered and enlightened Thai lady?

Upon closer inspection it became apparent that there was a different reason for Lah replacing Ralph at the yoga retreat. Lah had complained that Ralph was spending the money on himself, and later Ralph agreed to let her go instead. In fact Lah wanted to go so Ralph could not go.

At this point the sheen around this enlightened couple had tarnished. When Ralph was asked about the quality of his new age sex he appeared subdued. Ralph, who had always enjoyed oral sex before he met Lah, explained that his wife would not even allow him to use the words 'oral' and 'sex' in the same sentence. ...so it's back to the missionaries (see above).

## Case Study: Michael and his Lisu Girlfriend

Michael, a fifty-five-year-old American has a unique relationship with his forty-year-old Lisu girlfriend. He lives with her and her three children whenever he stays in Northern Thailand. Michael calls her 'The Jewel of the Forest' (Jewel), and she called him 'King'. Michael says Jewel really treats him like royalty and his time with her is blissful.

When Michael was forty-eight years old, he suffered a painful divorce in the States. Afterwards Michael travelled to Calcutta to witness other peoples' suffering before he arrived in Thailand, where he began his process of emotional healing.

Michael has no plans to marry again. He views marriage as a way for women to control their husbands. He believes the rubber stamp of marriage knocks the passion out from the present moment.

According to Michael, the relationship is perfect; communication between each other is mainly intuitive because they do not share a common language together. Jewel is illiterate, and can speak just a few words of the Thai and English languages.

They have no expectations of each other and they never argue. Michael describes the relationship as extremely 'hands on'; they love massaging each other and walking, cooking and eating together.

The colourful Lisu tribe from Kachin State and southern Shan State of Myanmar support themselves by hunting and cultivating crops. There are several Lisu villages scattered around Northern Thailand.

Jewel is mature, intuitive and kind. She is not possessive, so she allows Michael to do whatever he wants. She never gets jealous according to Michael. The couple does not try to change each other. Jewel, who is intimidated by Thai culture, has no desire to leave her neighbourhood.

The key to their relationship is simplicity and unconditional respect for one another, and neither partner tries to control or manipulate the other. They are both free to be themselves, living inter-dependently, rather than co-dependently.

No relationship is perfect; so for the sake of balance—here is an alternative viewpoint from a *farang* women:

'When you can't even talk to each other, I don't think you have a real relationship. It might be an easy way to have sex without getting very emotionally attached to someone because you were painfully hurt in the past—or it might be symbiotic in some way.

'Choosing a relationship partner who you cannot talk to is cheating, because you cannot deal with real issues; and you can never have an intellectual connection. You might as well be home alone with a bottle of lube, and a maid who cooks and cleans for you.

'I'd rather be alone than be with someone who doesn't get my jokes, can't discuss current events, and doesn't give me things to think about. If you aren't getting it (mind candy) from your 'partner' then you are getting it from somewhere else—your friends, her friends—cheating mentally, instead of physically.'

## THE PARADOX

Illuminated relationships are between people who are happy in their own right. Neither partner is dependent on the other person. The relationship is spiritual in essence.

If you need a relationship, you are not an enlightened being yet. The only truly illuminated relationship—cross cultural or otherwise—is with oneself.

## SIUMMARY

- The ancient Taoist philosophers have much knowledge to offer about healthy sexual relationships between men and women;
- Buddhist philosophy emphasizes that emotional attachment is the cause of pain and suffering.

# APPENDICES

# CONTACT DIRECTORY

| SOURCE | WEBSITE ADDRESS | DETAILS |
|---|---|---|
| Cross-Culture Relationships | CrossCultureLove.com | Relationship Contracts & Information |
| Embassies & Consulates | Embassyworld.com | Database of embassies worldwide |
| Financial Planning | Pfm-international.net | Legal & financial services for expats |
| Jerry Hopkins | Jerryhopkins.com | Thailand author |
| Ministry of Foreign Affairs | Mfa.go.th | Certification of Freedom To Marry Affidavit |
| Phil Nicks | Philnicks.com | Author's Website |
| Publishers | Monsoonbooks.com.sg Paiboonpublishing.com | Publishers of books relating to S.E. Asia |
| Stickman Bangkok | Stickmanbangkok.com | Articles about Thai-farang relationships |
| Thailand Visa Information | Thaivisa.com | Expat discussion groups |

# 'RAINFALL'
# by Toby Charnaud

*The following story was purportedly written by Toby Charnaud, shortly before he was murdered by his Thai spouse in 2005. For a summary of what actually happened, refer to 'The Farang Barbie' in the chapter 'Extreme Breakups'.*

Guy's fingers trembled as he lit yet another cigarette, the previous one still smouldering in the ashtray. His hands felt clammy and he was sweating, despite the chilling blast from the air-conditioning. There was a heavy feeling in the pit of his stomach. This was the most terrible thing he had done in his life, and the waiting was the hardest part.

He walked across to the window and stared out at the cityscape in front of him. Bangkok, shrouded in cloud. The rain had started and soon it would close in, relentless and oppressive. It rained hard like that the night he had met her, nearly three years ago.

He had been trawling through the bars of Soi Cowboy with Greg, a good friend and an old Bangkok hand. They had been out in the street flirting with the 'welcome' girls when the rain came, forcing them to take refuge on one of the bars.

It had been a standard go-go bar, and they had sat down on the bench seats around the outside and ordered a couple of beers. Half a dozen girls were dancing, their movements nothing more than going through the motions in time with the bland Thai pop music. One of the girls caught his eye. She was very petite, even for a Thai girl, with huge eyes. She smiled, a gorgeous lop-sided smile that lit up her whole face.

After her shift she came over, demurely holding out a dainty hand.

'Hello. My name Fon, may I sit down?'

He was taken with her politeness and her beauty. They laughed at the coincidence of her name and the random selection of the bar because of the rain, Fon being the Thai ward for rain. It was an omen and he was smitten.

He spent the rest of that trip with her, and the next one, contrived just a couple of months later. He had heard all the stories of how a relationship with a bargirl was doomed to fail. But those stories were not about Fon, she was different. Greg had tried to tell him that they all said that, 'this one is different', but he ignored him, and it was too late now.

Outside the rain closed in, the visibility dropped, the grey skies pushing in from all sides. He checked his wallet, the tickets were there, but there were still a couple of hours to go. There was an empty bottle of Mekong whisky on the table, maybe the last he would ever drink. He considered going to buy another, but couldn't face braving the downpour, and suddenly the thought of the cheap sweet taste made him feel sick.

He had known it would be difficult to get a visa for Fon to come to England, so had used the opportunity to do what he had dreamed about, to take off to pastures new. He sold his modest share portfolio and rented out his house and moved to Bangkok . He knew he would have no trouble finding a teaching job, but Greg was able to find him work in IT, to which he was more suited and paid far better.

Which, as it turned out, was no bad thing, as the problems with Fon started almost immediately. Nothing too much to begin with, and mostly about money. Then there was the not coming back to the apartment when she said, or coming back drunk. They would fight, she would cry, and then would smile with that extraordinary lop-sided smile and look at him with those huge eyes and he would forgive her. Always. As she knew he would.

But it didn't get better. There were more problems and more fights. They made the decision to move out of Bangkok. They went to Hua Hin on the gulf coast a couple of hours south. They found a suitable business available, a small bar and restaurant. Fon would run it and it would provide her with her own source of income. There was enough IT work available for Guy even in a town like Hua Hin. It seemed like the ideal solution.

Instead things soon got worse. It wasn't just the money, that was still as bad as ever, despite the business appearing to do well, but the lies started. Again they would fight and again she would cry and he would feel guilty.

He wanted to walk away, but couldn't, and her eyes would do their magic and he would take her into his arms.

Then came the stories of other men, customers in her bar, an old boyfriend from her Soi Cowboy days. He couldn't believe them and tried to ignore them, but on top of everything else it was too much. This time, when he confronted her, she became angry and denied everything. He believer her, he had to, he loved her too much and this time it had been his turn to back down and apologise.

While they lived in Hua Hin he got to know Boy. Boy was a tuk-tuk driver, a regular Thai guy. They would play pool together and talk football, and they became good friends. People told him that you shouldn't trust a Thai man, but Boy would never ask for money or accept any favours. He introduced him to his brother, Daeng. Daeng was a cop, not high ranking but with influence. He didn't have the same charm as Boy, and was always sponging drinks and chatting up the girls in the bar, who were very wary with him. However, he was a useful contact to have.

Then it happened. He caught Fon. He had gone to Bangkok to pick up some computer parts and had planned to have a night out with Greg, but Greg had been sick so he returned that evening. Fon was in a bed with this guy, a Dane, a regular customer in the bar. He didn't wait, he didn't want to hear. He left and three days later was back in England.

As soon as he arrived he started to miss Thailand, the food, the climate, the lifestyle. And he missed Fon. She called him constantly saying how sorry she was, what a mistake she had made, how she would never do it again, how much she loved him and how different it would be when he came back.

He held out for a short while, but he couldn't put her behind him. Every time he closed his eyes he saw that funny smile and those lovely, lovely eyes.

He went back. It got worse. He could not stop loving her, but she lied more and more, she cheated more and more. It was as if she knew that by getting him back, she had won. The though of leaving again, or just leaving her at all broke him up, but he knew that if he stayed she would destroy him.

Then it came to him. There was a way of dealing with this Thai-style. He spoke to Boy. Boy said he knew how to deal with it.

It was Boy he was waiting for now. It was too late to stop what he had put in motion, and although he had huge misgivings he was desperate and knew it was the only thing that he could do.

Beside the television there was a manila envelope. He opened it and counted the money again. 60,000 Baht. He had already paid 20,000 baht with the rest to be handed over when the job was done. Having paid for his airline tickets it was all the money he had left. He had been concerned about what would happen to Boy, but Daeng would take care of that. Perhaps he would have to spend a couple of months as a monk in a forest wat, but the disappearance of an Isaan peasant's daughter in a distant town would hardly be investigated and would soon be forgotten.

He looked out of the window. The rain had eased and the skies were lifting. Soon the sun would come out again. He stubbed out the cigarette and lit another one. Already he began to feel better.

There was a knock on the door. Peering through the spyhole he saw Boy. He looked relaxed; he hardly even looked wet. He opened the door to let him in.

Boy looked at him, his gaze steady.

'Finish' was all he said.

The heavy feeling in his stomach moved up to his heart and his eyes blurred. For the first time it was not just guilt or regret he felt but real remorse. He couldn't look at Boy and turned away to pick up the money.

'60,000.' He paused, 'I must go now Boy.'

Boy nodded as he took the cash.

'Take a good journey, my friend, 'he said.'

Guy forced himself to look up. His eyes widened with shock as

274

he saw the gun pointing at him. He didn't understand, couldn't take in what he saw. His last thought, bizarrely, was that the silencer was as big as the gun.

The girl slipped into the room. She was tiny with large brown eyes. She looked at the body on the floor, then at the man slipping the gun back into the waistband of his jeans. The expression on her face was of regret, sorrow and bewilderment. It passed quickly and she turned to Boy.

'Come on, tilac, let's go,' he said.

She gave him a quick lop-sided smile and took his hand as they left the room.

# SAMPLE CONTRACTS

1. Usufruct Contract
2. Prenuptial Agreement
3. Sample Freedom To Marry Affidavit

# **Usufruct Contract**
# **สัญญาให้สิทธิเก็บกิน**

*This contract is signed at household number ............. Moo ...... Tambon ......, Amphur............, Province................, Thailand on ............... between..........................., holder of Thai Identification number ......................... of .....(Address)..... herein after will be called the "OWNER".*

สัญญาฉบับนี้จัดทำขึ้นที่ บ้านเลขที่ ..... หมู่ที่ ..... ตำบล ............ อำเภอ ............ จังหวัด ............ เมื่อวันที่ ............ ระหว่าง ..................................... ผู้ถือบัตรประจำตัว ประชาชนไทยเลขที่ ........................................ พำนักอยู่บ้านเลขที่ ........(ที่อยู่)...... ซึ่งต่อไปในสัญญานี้จะเรียกว่า **"เจ้าของ"** ฝ่ายหนึ่ง

*And ................., ............ National, passport number .........................., of .....(Address)..... herein after will be called the "HOLDER OF RIGHT".*

กับ.................................สัญชาติ....................ถือหนังสือเดินทางเลขที่ ................................. พำนักอยู่บ้านเลขที่ ........(ที่อยู่)...... ซึ่งต่อไปในสัญญานี้จะเรียกว่า **"ผู้ทรงสิทธิ"** อีกฝ่ายหนึ่ง

The owner is holding the ownership of the land title deed number ............ Land Number ............ Front Survey Number ............, Tambon ............, Amphur ............, ............, Thailand. Total Land size ............ Rai ............ Ngan ............ Talang Wa, stated in attachment number 1, herein after will be called "PROPERTY".

โดยที่เจ้าของถือครองกรรมสิทธิ์ในที่ดิน ฉโนดเลขที่ ............ เลขที่ดิน ............ หน้าสำรวจ ............ ตำบล............ อำเภอ............ จังหวัด............ ซึ่งมีเนื้อที่ทั้งหมด ............ ไร่ ............ งาน ............ ตารางวา ดังแสดงในเอกสารหมายเลขที่ 1 แนบท้ายสัญญานี้ ซึ่ง ต่อไปในสัญญานี้จะเรียกว่า **"ทรัพย์สิน"**

Both parties are agreed on the following conditions:
ทั้งสองฝ่ายได้ตัดลงทำสัญญากัน โดยมีข้อความดังต่อไปนี้ :

**No.1** The owner agrees to give the holder of right the usufruct to possess and use the benefit from the property including the power to manage entire of the property.
**ข้อ 1.** เจ้ายินยอมให้ผู้ทรงสิทธิมีสิทธิเก็บกินในทรัพย์สิน โดยให้มีสิทธิจะครอบครองใช้สอยและ ถือเอาซึ่งประโยชน์จากทรัพย์สินดังกล่าว ตลอดทั้งให้มีอำนาจในการจัดการทรัพย์สินทั้งหมด

**No. 2** The usufruct stated in clause number 1 is for life time of the holder of right started from the completion of this contract.

**ข้อ 2.** สิทธิเก็บกินตามข้อ 1 เป็นการให้สิทธิเก็บกินตลอดชีวิตของผู้ทรงสิทธินับแต่วันทำสัญญา

**No. 3** The usufruct agreed in this contract will expire when the holder of the rights is dead.

**ข้อ 3.** ในกรณีที่ผู้ทรงสิทธิถึงแก่ความตาย ให้ถือว่าสิทธิเก็บกินตามสัญญานี้เป็นอันระงับสิ้นไป

**No. 4** The utilization of the usufruct property, the holder of right agrees to maintain and protect the property as his property.

**ข้อ 4.** ในการใช้สิทธิเก็บกินนั้น ผู้ทรงสิทธิต้องรักษาทรัพย์สินเสมอกับที่วิญญูชนจะพึงรักษา ทรัพย์สินของตนเอง

**No. 5** The holder of right can transfer his usufruct to another party without permission from the owner.

**ข้อ 5.** ผู้ทรงสิทธิจะโอนสิทธิเก็บกินไปให้ผู้อื่นหรือบุคคลภายนอกได้โดยไม่จำเป็นต้องได้รับ ความยินยอมเป็นลายลักษณ์อักษรจากเจ้าของ

**No. 6** The holder of right can not use the property for any illegal purposes.

**ข้อ 6.** ผู้ทรงสิทธิจะใช้ทรัพย์สินในทางอันมิชอบด้วยกฎหมายไม่ได้

**No. 7** The holder of right is responsible for the management of the property, including payment of all taxes relating to the property, loans, and interest charges over the property.

**ข้อ 7.** ผู้ทรงสิทธิต้องออกค่าใช้จ่ายในการจัดการทรัพย์สิน ตลอดจนค่าภาษีอากรอันเกี่ยวกับ ทรัพย์สิน รวมทั้งต้องใช้ดอกเบี้ยหนี้สินซึ่งติดพันทรัพย์สินนั้น

**No. 8** Both parties agree to sign this contract free of profit between each parties (non-profit).

**ข้อ 8.** สัญญาให้สิทธิเก็บกินฉบับนี้คู่สัญญาได้ตกลงและจัดทำขึ้นโดยไม่มีวัตถุประสงค์เพื่อ มุ่งหวังค่าตอบแทนแต่อย่างใด

This is a three pages English – Thai contract, of which 2 copies have been made in equal substance and effect. Prior to signing this contract in front of witnesses, both parties have read and understood clearly the entire contents of this contract and agreed to be bound by it. It is understood that both parties will keep one copy of the signed contract.

หนังสือสัญญาฉบับนี้ทำขึ้นเป็นภาษาอังกฤษและภาษาไทยจำนวนทั้งสิ้นสองฉบับ ฉบับละสาม หน้าซึ่งมีข้อความถูกต้องตรงกัน ทั้งสองฝ่ายได้อ่านและเข้าใจข้อความในสัญญาโดยตลอดแล้ว จึง ลงลายมือชื่อไว้เป็นสำคัญต่อหน้าพยาน

Signature...................................Owner   Signature
.........................Usufructuary

(...............................)                    (...............................)

Date......Month............Year...........
Date.....Month............Year...........


Signature................................... Witness   Signature .........................
Witness

(...............................)                    (...............................)

Date......Month............Year...........
Date......Month............Year...........

**DISCLAIMER**
**THIS SPECIMEN CONTRACT IS FOR REFERENCE PURPOSES ONLY**

# Prenuptial Agreement

## สัญญาก่อนสมรส

- ADDRESS -

- ที่อยู่ -

This prenuptial agreement is entered into on the .......... day of ..........month, Year..........

สัญญาก่อนสมรสฉบับนี้ได้จัดทำขึ้นและสมบูรณ์เมื่อวันที่..........เดือน.................... ปี พ.ศ. ..........

(1) "Prenuptial Agreement" means an agreement between prospective spouses made in contemplation of marriage and to be effective upon marriage.

"สัญญาก่อนสมรส" หมายถึง สัญญาระหว่างคู่สมรสในอนาคต โดยมีเจตนาเพื่อการสมรสและเพื่อให้มีผลบังคับใช้ต่อไปในชีวิตการสมรสของคู่สัญญา

(2) "Property" means an interest, present or future, legal or equitable, vested or contingent, in real or personal property, including income and earnings.

"ทรัพย์สิน" หมายถึง ผลประโยชน์ ทั้งที่มีอยู่ในปัจจุบันและในอนาคต ทั้งที่มีอยู่โดยถูกต้องตามกฎหมายและเป็นธรรม ซึ่งได้ครอบครองไว้โดยชอบธรรมหรือไม่ก็ตาม ทั้งสังหาหรืออสังหาริมทรัพย์ ทรัพย์สินส่วนตัว รวมถึงรายได้ต่างๆ

**Between – ระหว่าง:**

The "Prospective Husband", .........(name)............, .........(nationality)............ national, bearer of passport number ................., date of birth ................, of .....(Address)..... herein after to be called "............." and

"ว่าที่สามี" .......(ชื่อ)....... สัญชาติ..... ผู้ถือหนังสือเดินทางเลขที่ ................ เกิดวันที่ ............... ภูมิลำเนาอยู่ที่..... (ที่อยู่)....... ซึ่งต่อไปในสัญญานี้จะเรียกว่า "..........." และ

The "Prospective Wife", .........(name)............ , ......(nationality)...... national, date of birth .................... bearer of Thai identification card number..................... of, Thailand here in after to be called "............."

"ว่าที่ภรรยา" .......(ชื่อ)....... สัญชาติ................ เกิดวันที่ .... เดือน.......... พ.ศ. ......... ผู้ถือ
บัตรประจำตัวประชาชนชาวไทยเลขที่ ..................... ภูมิลำเนาอยู่บ้านเลขที่ ...................
(ที่อยู่)........................... ซึ่งต่อไปในสัญญานี้จะเรียกว่า "................."

The parties wish to clarify estates whatsoever and wheresoever, both real and personal in and outside of Thailand the present respective financial interests before their marriage.

คู่สัญญาประสงค์ที่จะแถลงทรัพย์สินก่อนสมรสและผลประโยชน์ของตนไม่ว่าจะเป็นสังหาหรือ
อสังหาริมทรัพย์    ทั้งในประเทศไทยและต่างประเทศ

Now, therefore, it is agreed as followed:

ทั้งสองฝ่ายได้ตกลง ดังต่อไปนี้:

1. Both parties agreed that the law of Kingdom of Thailand and the law of the ..................., shall be applied in any circumstance of their marrigage.

   คู่สัญญาทั้งสองฝ่ายได้ตกลงให้การสมรสของตนอยู่ภายใต้บังคับ        กฎหมายของ
   ราชอาณาจักรไทย และกฎหมายของ........................ ในทุกกรณี

2. The personal assets owned by ........ before the marriage will remain his exclusive property, including appreciation in value after marriage, the right to buy, sell, use, transfer, exchange, abandon, lease, consume, expend, assign, create a security interest in, mortgage, encumber, dispose of, or otherwise manage and control property. ........... has disclosed to ........., all of his personal assets (See Appendix A)............

   ทรัพย์สินก่อนสมรสที่ถือครองโดย ........... ยังคงเป็นกรรมสิทธิ์ของ........... และคงสิทธิใน
   การครอบครอง ดูแลทรัพย์สินของตน อาทิ สิทธิในการซื้อ ขาย ใช้ประโยชน์ โอน
   แลกเปลี่ยน ละทิ้ง ให้เช่า ใช้อุปโภค บริโภค ขยาย สร้างหลักความมั่นคงให้แก่
   ผลประโยชน์ในทรัพย์สิน จำนอง ภาระ การย้ายออก หรือ การจัดการ หรือควบคุมใด ๆ
   เหนือ ทรัพย์สิน ซึ่ง ........... ได้แจ้งให้ ........... ทราบแล้ว ดังมีรายละเอียดทรัพย์สิน
   ก่อนสมรส ระบุไว้ใน *ภาคผนวก ก*

3. The personal assets owned by ........ before the marriage will remain her exclusive property, including appreciation in value after marriage, the right to buy, sell, use, transfer, exchange, abandon, lease, consume, expend, assign, create a security interest in, mortgage, encumber, dispose of, or otherwise

manage and control property. ............ has disclosed to ........., all of his personal assets (See Appendix B)............

ทรัพย์สินก่อนสมรสที่ถือครองโดย ........... ยังคงเป็นกรรมสิทธิ์ของ........... และคงสิทธิใน การครอบครอง ดูแลทรัพย์สินของตน อาทิ สิทธิในการซื้อ ขาย ใช้ประโยชน์ โอน แลกเปลี่ยน ละทิ้ง ให้เช่า ใช้อุปโภค บริโภค ขยาย สร้างหลักความมั่นคงให้แก่ ผลประโยชน์ในทรัพย์สิน จำนอง ภาระ การย้ายออก หรือ การจัดการ หรือควบคุมใด ๆ เหนือ ทรัพย์สิน ซึ่ง ........... ได้แจ้งให้ ........... ทราบแล้ว ดังมีรายละเอียดทรัพย์สิน ก่อนสมรส ระบุไว้ใน *ภาคผนวก ข*

4. If the marriage is ended, discontinue or come to an end in any circumstance, legally or practically. It is agreed that ..... shall received his/her compensation from ......, in cash or asset, in equivalent to duration of marriage;

หากการสมรสสิ้นสุด หรือยุติลง ไม่ว่าจะด้วยเหตุใดก็ตาม ไม่ว่าจะโดยผลของกฎหมาย หรือในทางปฏิบัติ คู่สัญญาทั้งสองฝ่ายได้ตกลงกันว่า ....... จะมอบเงินสด หรือ ทรัพย์สิน เพื่อเป็นค่าชดเชย ซึ่งมีมูลค่าขึ้นอยู่กับระยะเวลาการสมรสของทั้งสองฝ่าย ให้แก่ ..............

However, in no event will the payment to ..... exceed .... percent of the total net assets owned by ........ at the date of divorce.

อย่างไรก็ตาม จะไม่มีกรณีใด ๆ ที่ค่าชดเชยดังกล่าว ที่ ...... พึงได้รับจะมีจำนวนเกินกว่า ..... เปอร์เซ็นต์ ของทรัพย์สินทั้งหมดที่ ..... เป็นเจ้าของ และถือครองอยู่ ณ วันที่มีการหย่าเกิดขึ้น

5. After marriage, a preneptial agreement may be amended or revoked only by a written agreement signed by both parties. The amended agreement or the revocation is enforceable without consideration.

สัญญาก่อนสมรสฉบับนี้ อาจจะมีการเปลี่ยนแปลงหรือยกเลิกได้หลังจากการสมรสแล้ว โดยทำเป็น ลายลักษณ์อักษร และลงนามโดยคู่สัญญาทั้งสองฝ่าย สัญญาก่อนสมรส ที่ได้รับการแก้ไขดังกล่าว มีผลบังคับใช้ได้ทันที

However, If a marriage is determined to be void, an agreement that would otherwise have been a premarital agreement is enforceable only to the extent necessary to avoid an inequitable result.

อย่างไรก็ดี หากการสมรสนี้เป็นโมฆะ ข้อตกลงต่าง ๆ ในสัญญาฉบับนี้ ให้ถือมีผลบังคับ ใช้ได้ในทางที่จะคุ้มครองคู่สัญญาในกรณีที่อาจเกิดความไม่เสมอภาคใด ๆ ขึ้น

This Premarital Agreement is made in Thai and English, two copies have been made. All copies are of equal substance and effect. The parties have checked that all statements in this document are as per their intention. Both parties have fully understood the agreement before duly signing in front of the witnesses.

สัญญาก่อนสมรสฉบับนี้จัดทำขึ้นเป็นภาษาไทยและภาษาอังกฤษ จำนวนทั้งสิ้นสองฉบับ ซึ่งมีข้อความถูกต้องตรงกัน คู่สัญญาทั้งสองฝ่ายได้อ่าน และตรวจสอบข้อความในสัญญาบับนี้แล้ว และเข้าใจในรายละเอียดข้อตกลง และคู่สัญญาทั้งสองฝ่ายเห็นแล้วว่าตรงตามความต้องการของตน จึงได้ลงนามต่อหน้าพยาน

**Prospective Husband – ว่าที่สามี**

Signature-ลงชื่อ_____

Print full name-ลายมือชื่อ_____

Date of signature-วันที่ลงนาม: _____

_____

**Prospective Wife-ว่าที่ภรรยา**

Signature-ลงชื่อ_____

Print full name-ลายมือชื่อ_____

Date of signature-วันที่ลงนาม: _____

_____

We who act as witnesses do hereby confirm that both parties ................................, the Prospective Husband and,........................., the Prospective Wife, are in fill command of their mind and are not subject to duress, fraud or undue influence and did indeed sign in our presence with clear intentions.

ข้าพเจ้าทั้งหลายผู้เป็นพยาน ขอยืนยันว่า คู่สัญญาทั้งสองฝ่าย ได้แก่ .....................ว่าที่สามี และ ........................ว่าที่ภรรยา มีสติสัมปชัญญะสมบูรณ์ และดำเนินการโดยปราศจากการถูกหลอกลวง ฉ้อฉล หรือถูกบังคับ ข่มขู่ใด ๆ และ ได้ลงนามต่อหน้าข้าพเจ้าทั้งหลายด้วยความตั้งใจจริง

**First Witness -พยานคนที่ 1:**

_____

Signature-ลงชื่อ

_____

Print full name-ลายมือชื่อ

_____

Date of signature-วันที่ลงนาม:

**Second Witness-พยานคนที่ 2:**

_____

Signature-ลงชื่อ

_____

Print full name-ลายมือชื่อ

_____

Date of signature-วันที่ลงนาม:

## SAMPLE FREEDOM TO MARRY AFFIDAVIT

I, ...................(full name )................holder of (country) Passport No. .................... issued at .......... on .................. and valid until .................... make oath and declare as follows: -

I am a ..........citizen and I was born on ................ in .................... My father's name is ........................... and my mother's name is ...... ...............................

I am not bound by the ties of a lawful marriage under the laws of .....................(country) and I am free to contract a valid marriage with .................................... ( name and details of person ) according to Thai law.

I am single and have not previously been married / I am widowed / divorced. (*)

(please attach appropriate certificates - originals only )

I have no dependents from my previous marriage(s). (*)

I support ................ children from my previous marriage(s). (*)

My occupation is ........................... and I have an income of .......... per month as proof of which I attach an employer's letter / bank statement ( for Thai Authorities only )

I propose the following people for reference purposes if it is necessary to verify the above details:

1. Name ..........................................................

Address ........................................................

2. Name ..........................................................

Address ........................................................

(It is usually preferable that these people live in the same country as the signatory. Parents may be referees)

My permanent address is .....................................................

Sworn before me at the ................ Embassy / Consulate in Bangkok in

Thailand this ......... day of ............................

Honorary Consul
(*) Delete as appropriate

# AMPHUR OFFICES IN THAILAND

1. Khet Pathumwan Registration Office
216/1 Chula 7, Kwang Wang-Mai, Bangkok 10330
Tel: 02-214-3004

2. Khet Prakhanong Registration Office
1792 Sukhumvit Soi 54, Kwang Bangjak, Bangkok 10250
Tel: 02-311-1107

3. Khet Bangrak Registration Office
5 Nares Road , Kwang Siphraya, Bangkok 10500
Tel: 02-236-1395

4. Amphur Koh Samui Registration Office
Taweeraj Pakdee Road , Tambon Angtong, Amphur Kok Samui,
Surat Thani 84140
Tel: 077-420-372, 420-373

5. Amphur Muang Phuket Registration Office
Mae-Larn Road , Tambon Talardyai, Amphur Muang, Phuket
83000
Tel: 076-211-171

6. Amphur Muang Chiang Mai Registration Office
36 Intavarorot Road , Tambon Sri-Poom, Amphur Muang,
Chiang Mai 50000
Tel: 053-221-016

7. Amphur Banglamung Registration Office
Moo 2, Sukhumvit Road , Tambon Na Klua, Amphur
Banglamung,
Chonburi 20150
Tel: 038-443-020

8. Hua Him District Office
Dumnoenkasem Road , Hua Hin, Prachuap Khiri Khan 77110
Tel: 032-511-025, 512-267

9. Amphur Koh Phangan
Moo 2 Tongsala Chaloklum Road , Tambon Koh Phangan,
Suratthani 84280
Tel: 077-377-021, 377-064

10. Krabi Registration Office
Uttarakij Road , Tambon Paknam, Amphur Muang,
Krabi 81000
Tel: 075-611-340

# GLOSSARY OF TERMS

| | |
|---|---|
| *Amphur* office | Municipal office |
| Bargirl | Obliging and commercially-oriented lady (not to be confused with the Western concept of prostitution) |
| *Butprachachun* | Identity card |
| *Farang* | Foreigner |
| *Gig* | Partner for casual sexual relationship |
| *Greng jai* | Avoiding confrontation |
| *Jaochoo* | Multiple relationships |
| *Katoey* | Ladyboy |
| *Ki neow* | Stingy |
| *Koo mun* | Engaged |
| *Mahu* | Hawaiian ladyboy |
| *Mia noi* | Second 'little' wife (mistress) |
| *Porsoo* | Third-party mediator |
| *Sinsod* | Dowry |
| *Tabian baan* | Household registration |
| *Thong mun* | Engagement gift (of gold) |

# ACKNOWLEDGEMENTS

The author wishes to thank everyone who provided assistance to this project, especially: Alan Hall, Andrew Weller, Barry Sandal, Cat Miller, Chantana 'Mem' Jasper, Siobhan Smith, Chris Pirazzi, Jerry Hopkins, Ken Albertsen, Ken Klein, Liza Day, Terry Lee, Thomas Brittner, Waan Supaparinya, Warren Olson, Phil Tatham, Alan from Hawaii, Mark E Smith, James Bradley and Laddawan.

# REFERENCES

'Are you Man enough to be a Woman?' By Sanitsuda Ekachai, *Bangkok Post*, 1 October 2007

*Building a House in Thailand*, Ken Klein, White Lotus Co., Ltd

*Confessions of A Bangkok Private Eye: True stories from the case files of Warren Olson*, Warren Olson, Monsoon Books

*Culture Shock! Thailand*, Robert & Nanthapa Cooper, Marshall Cavendish Editions

*Foreign Relations: A Comic Guide to Thai Ladies*, Barry Sandal

*From Condoms to Cabbages: An Authorized Biography of Mechai Viravaidya*, Thomas D'Agnes, Post Books

*Good Medicine for Thailand Fever: A Roadmap for Thai-Western Relationships*, Chris Pirazzi & Vitida Vasant, Paiboon Publishing

*Guru Magazine* ('Love Rules' by Yanisa @ Midas-PR, Articles by Nikki @ Meet 'N' Lunch)

'How do we Measure Up?' The results of a sex survey of ACPG readers in Thailand, Hong Kong and Singapore, Gregoire Glachant, *BK Magazine* 20-26 April 2007

*How To Establish A Successful Business In Thailand*, Philip Wylie, Paiboon Publishing

'Investigative Interviewing of Asians by New Zealand Agencies', by Warren Olson (a research paper completed in conjunction with a degree in strategic studies, undertaken at the School of Government,

Victoria University, Wellington, New Zealand, 2007)

*Lali's Passage ~ Burmese Beauty escapes from Brothel to Native American Hills of California*, Ken Albertsen, Sabaibooks.com

'Online Dating', 'Surfing the Web for Mr Right', 'Educated Women of Rural Origin', 'Widows Seek Foreign Spouse', Kamol Sukin, *The Nation*, 12 August 2007

*Pocket Thailand in Figures*, Alpha Research Co., Ltd

*Private Dancer*, Stephen Leather, Monsoon Books

*Sex Slaves: The trafficking of women in Asia*, Louise Brown, Little, Brown & Company (UK)

*Singapore Girl: A Memoir*, James Eckardt, Monsoon Books

*The Tao of Health, Sex and Longevity*, Daniel Reid, Simon & Schuster

*Thai Girl*, Andrew Hicks, Monsoon Books

*Thai Law For Foreigners*, Benjawan Poomsan Becker, Paiboon Publishing

*Warning: Sex May be Hazardous to your Health*, Dr Edwin Flatto, Arco Publishing Company

*Why Men Don't Listen and Women can't Read Maps*, Barbara and Allan Pease, Broadway Books

# INDEX